Uncle Mendy

AN AMERICAN LIFE

by
MENDEL BLUMBERG

as told to his nephew
DAVID SCHWARTZ

STICKY EARTH BOOKS

Also by David Schwartz

A VIP Day at Independence Park
A day behind the scenes with a Volunteer-In-Parks at Independence National Historical Park

Elsewhere Than Vietnam
A Story of the Sixties

COPYRIGHT © 2021 David Schwartz

Published By
STICKY EARTH BOOKS
Exton, Pennsylvania

ALL RIGHTS RESERVED

THIS BOOK OR any portion thereof may not be reproduced or used in any manner whatsoever without the express written permission of the copyright owner except for the use of brief quotations in a book review.

Paperback ISBN 978-0-9986449-8-1

Library Of Congress Control Number: 2021949252

*To all of our family members
of the Greatest Generation.*

Table of Contents

Foreword 1

My Youth 5

The War Years 33

From Claremont to Florida 57

Life on the Back Stretch 71

A Courier On His Appointed Rounds 79

Retirement Years 89

Encore 103

My Own Ticket 109

Afterword 117

About The Author 123

Foreword

WHEN I WAS growing up, Uncle Mendy was always a bit of a mystery to me. He lived in Florida, far away from the rest of the family, but was a periodic presence in my life on his trips north.

My father, my uncles, and a couple of aunts had served in the military in World War II. My mother's other brother, David, had been killed in the fighting in France after the D-Day invasion of Normandy. I was named after him.

I gathered from my mother that Mendy's service had been especially tough. He had fought in many battles. She didn't know the details — nobody did — because Mendy never talked about it.

Mendy was extraordinarily private about his personal life too. Nobody knew of any women in it. When he came north each year to attend his Army reunions and family occasions like weddings, he came alone.

Uncle Mendy was a bachelor: handsome and charming, a meticulous dresser, and tan from the Florida sun. Unlike my father and uncles who worked in offices and commuted to New York City, Mendy was a mailman and worked outdoors. By mid-afternoon on most days, he would be finished with work and go play golf. He was the best golfer in the family. He loved music. He lived a free life which he seemed to enjoy to the fullest.

My brother Dan and I tormented our mother by telling her that when we grew up, we wanted to be just like Uncle Mendy.

He had a compelling personality: engaging, humorous, filled with knowledge he was willing to share. During one visit he taught me how to tie my shoelaces. He was a storyteller and spoke to us nephews and nieces as if we were older. He leveled with us.

He was wonderfully knowledgeable about sports. An avid Red Sox fan, he regaled Dan and me with stories of baseball in the glory decades of Babe Ruth and Ted Williams. As we threw a baseball back and forth, he gave pointers on the proper way to use a baseball glove and how to care for its leather with glove oil.

Beginning around 2005, I began to take a business trip to Florida each January to meet with a client in Vero Beach. I started the practice of leaving a day early and flying in to West Palm Beach so I could spend an afternoon and evening with Mendy. We would have dinner – early – at one of his favorite chain restaurants, then watch some sports on TV at his apartment. We would have breakfast together the next morning at his diner, and then I would be on my way. On one trip I got him talking about his war experiences. Back in my Holiday Inn room that night I wrote down notes of everything I could remember that he told me.

The next year, at dinner at Outback or Olive Garden, I got him started again talking about the war. I confessed to him that I had taken notes the previous year, and that I wanted to write down his whole autobiography as he would tell it to me. He was not interested. I said that all the family members of my generation would cherish having it. He finally agreed to do it, but on one condition: nobody should see it until after his death. "I don't want to have to answer any questions," he said.

That began our time of "working on the manuscript", as he called it. We talked on my visits and on phone calls. He went through his life year by year. He had a terrific memory. I would type pages from my notes and mail them to Mendy. He would mark up the pages in red ink with his corrections and mail them back to me.

This is his autobiography, in his voice, as he told it to me.

Fannie and Minnie Klein, 1910

1
My Youth

I WAS BORN in the small town of Ft. Kent, Maine, on September 26, 1919, to Meyer Blumberg and Minnie Klein Blumberg. Ft. Kent is located at the northern tip of Maine across the St. John River from Canada. We lived there until I was around four years old. My father, a rabbi, had come from Lithuania. His home town had been Swiechiany, about 50 miles from Vilnius, the provincial capital. He had been recruited there to come to Ft. Kent to serve its Jewish congregation of maybe 20 families in the area. A lot of members of the Klein family lived there, and my father married Minnie Klein.

Minnie's sister, my aunt Fannie Klein, lived there and had already married Abe Gray, an itinerant peddler of dry goods. Abe had been living in Chelsea, Massachusetts around 1910 when half the town burned down, affecting his business. He heard that business was good in northern Maine, so he took his horse and buggy and dry goods to Ft. Kent.

My mother's name in Lithuania had been Shimolevitz. At Ellis Island, the immigrants would ask the immigration officials for a "kleine" — meaning short — name. So they were assigned the name of Klein, like so many others. The Grovonsky's became the "Grays." My father's name was Brumberg, and it was just changed to "Blumberg", showing that the officials could almost handle just two syllables.

Mendy, Meyer "Papa", Rose, Minnie, Dorothy, 1921

They started me in the first grade in school when I was three years old. My sister Rose was in the second grade, and both grades shared the same classroom. When I had to go to the bathroom, I did not know the correct protocol, so I just stood up and walked out without asking the teacher.

The teacher gave Rose a note to take home to our parents that noon, suggesting that they keep me at home for another year.

There was a one-room shul (synagogue) next to the house, and an outhouse in the back. On holidays the shul was jam packed with people from all the surrounding towns. We had a cow tethered across the street. I remember once running after the car that was taking my father, who was also the shochet (ritual butcher), to the slaughterhouse. I was crying because I wanted to go with them.

Our house was on the bank of the river. There was no bridge across the river, only a small ferry that was really just a raft, operated by ropes pulled from either riverbank. A new engine-powered ferry was bought to replace it, and the dedication was to be on the Fourth of July, just 100 yards up the river from our house. After the festivities, we watched the new ferry move out 10 or 15 yards into the water and promptly sink.

The St. John River froze over in winter. Since this was during Prohibition, the Kleins and the Grays took nighttime excursions across the ice on horse-drawn sleighs to buy booze in Canada. At least once I was all bundled up and made the trip.

In 1923, we moved to the small factory town of Claremont, New Hampshire. Our house was on Central Street at the bottom of a hill. The front part of the house facing the street was the shul, and behind it were the living room, dining room and kitchen. There was no electricity in the kitchen at first, and light came from gas lamps with cloth wicks lit by matches. Electricity was soon installed in the kitchen. There was a large walk-in pantry, and a shed which served as an icebox in winter. The original stove burned coal, but then we converted to an oil burning stove that used a five-gallon jug of oil. We had a large 100-gallon hot water heater. Upstairs, over the shul, was a big bedroom, and then a larger bedroom in the center. These two bedrooms, for my sisters Rose, Dorothy, Celia, and Rachael, had radiators.

Claremont, NH 1920

My brother David and I shared a double bed in a small bedroom over the kitchen. Our bedroom had no heat. There was only a metal grate which during the day let in warm air rising up from the kitchen. I had a thermometer in our bedroom — during the day in the winter it would get up to

40 degrees; at night sometimes it could drop down to 15 or 20 degrees. Our neighbor used to make us warm blankets. We had long walk-in closets, but we owned almost nothing to put in them.

There was one bathroom in the house by the stairs, adjacent to my bedroom. It had a bathtub with a hose with showerhead hooked up. Down the stairs in the cellar was the furnace, the coal bin, and the mikvah (ritual bath). The stairs to the upstairs and down to the cellar were between the shul and the living room.

The shul normally had a single row of chairs and school desks where my father taught Hebrew school. On holidays 60 to 70 more chairs were brought in to accommodate the 30 or so Jewish families in town and the vicinity. The nearest towns with other congregations were Keene and Concord, both 50 miles away.

A covered walkway led from the kitchen porch out to the barn. In the barn there was the chicken coop on one side, then an open area, which later we made into our basketball court, and then the grocery store and meat market which my father ran. There was a large 6-door refrigerator for the store which used ice in the summer, but needed nothing in the winter. A vegetable garden ran the whole length of the property in back of the house. Gardening was my father's hobby. He grew corn, lettuce, tomatoes, cucumbers, carrots, radishes, peas and string beans. We also got corn from our milk lady at 10 cents a dozen. We had two pear trees, two apple trees, and a butternut tree. Squirrels loved the butternuts and stored them away for the winter.

My mother Minnie died in August, 1925 at the age of 36, when I was almost 6 years old. My memory of my mother is hazy, and I don't remember much about her. She suffered from post-partum depression after the birth of her sixth child, and she went away to the Brattleboro Retreat, a sanitarium. I remember travelling there once with my father, but I don't remember if I actually saw her. There she contracted an infection or inflammation of the heart which proved fatal.

In addition to our shul, there were four churches on Central Street: Methodist, Catholic with convent and school, Unitarian, and one other. Most of our neighbors were French Canadian. Our next-door neighbors were the Gellis family. Mr. Gellis owned gas stations and sent his son Sidney to Harvard, and his daughters to Radcliff and Cornell. Sidney subscribed to The Crimson for me, the Harvard weekly newspaper which came every Friday. From then on I became an avid Harvard sports fan.

The elementary school was a 5-minute walk away in the Bluff, a more affluent neighborhood. In grades 1 through 4, we walked home for lunch every day. I owned one pair of shoes, one pair of school pants, and my pair of old pants from the previous year. After school I would change my pants and put on the old pants to play in. I wore knickers up until high school, and I did get a suit for my bar mitzvah. I owned one toy — a Tinker Toy, which came with an illustrated manual of things for me to build with them. A step up from a Tinker Toy was the Erector Set, but I never had one.

Mendy

All we did was play ball, and games like Kick the Can, Red Rover and Hide and Seek. Our yard was big enough for baseball — a good hit went across the street. In the fall we played football on the back lawn. I had a pair of skis, so at lunchtime I skied home down the hill and curved into the dirt driveway. One time I crashed into the house and broke both skis. I also did a lot of cross-country skiing, in the woods near the Bluff. Our method of removing snow from the driveway was to wait for April.

I got a baseball glove when I was in 7th grade. It was a Huey Ritz model. He was the second baseman for the Giants. It cost two or three dollars. When I was a freshman, I tried out for the baseball team. Maybe 15 or 20 kids in the school had gloves, and we passed them around among the players. I didn't make the team.

We spent every summer playing sandlot baseball. We had found a field on the outskirts of town, measured out 90 feet for each base path, and 60 feet 6 inches from home plate to the pitcher's mound. We mowed the field with a borrowed mower, and this eventually became our baseball field.

I subscribed to The Sporting News, a baseball weekly, which carried the box scores of the major and even minor league teams. So I knew all the Red Sox minor leaguers and followed their progress up to the major leagues, including the young Ted Williams.

We made a basketball court in the barn. We nailed up a metal can and played with a tennis ball. Some of the kids waiting for class with Papa would play with us while they were waiting. There were three brothers, all eventually over six feet tall, who got their training in the barn and later all played on the high school varsity team. We also pitched horseshoes in the yard, and I was pretty good.

When I was around 10 or 11 years old, some of the guys in town in their 20's and 30's formed a YMHA, in order that they could have a club basketball team to play other club teams. They made me their ball boy and mascot. I was given a small blue and white team uniform to wear. We played at St. Jean's Hall at the top of the hill, which belonged to a church, since we had no gym of our own. I had plenty of time when they were not using one of the baskets to practice my own shooting skills. This was the beginning of my development as a sharpshooter.

I went to the library a lot. In the kids' section I started at one end and went row by row methodically checking out every book that interested me. In the summer I would take out four or five books a week and read them. I would even read walking home from the library, so engrossed in the books that I didn't even remember the walk. My feet just took me home like a dog who knew the way. I liked the historical novels of Joseph Altschuler, who wrote about the Revolutionary War and the Civil War.

When I finished all the books I wanted in the kids' section, I started on the adult section. I could read a book a day in the hammock on the porch. At night I had a flashlight for reading in bed until I built my lamp in the 7th grade. Accordingly, I never had a problem with book reports.

My teachers were Miss Abbott in second grade, Miss Sullinger in third grade (she was also the principal), and Miss Fry in fourth grade (a redhead). We would line up at the blackboard for a spelling bee, and I was often the last one standing. There were three reading groups one year: the Sparrows, the Robins, and for the most advanced readers, the Bluebirds. My friend Harry Barker took me home one day and introduced me with "Mom, this is Mendel

Bluebird." We went to school no matter what the weather, trudging through a foot or foot and a half of snow. In winter, there was a horse-drawn plow the width of the sidewalk which cleared the sidewalks. The factories blew their whistles on the rare days that school was closed to let us know.

The whole family always ate all meals together, except for breakfast. We ate well since Papa owned the grocery store. Friday and Saturday meals were special. On the Sabbath, a kid from across the street would come turn our lights on and off and turn on the stove, since the Orthodox rules forbid us to do that.

We were the only family in town who did not go to school on all of the many Jewish holidays. Papa was orthodox Orthodox. We accepted all the religious observances as normal. We took our school work home before the holidays and did it at home. For Passover, a salesman would come around and Papa ordered maybe a dozen items that were kosher for Passover, which were all there were back then. He also ordered a box full of fish from a fishery in Boston with which to make gefilte fish. I was the fish chopper, using a double-bladed chopper in a wooden bowl.

The store was stocked with Passover food and Manischewitz wine. Papa would put breadcrumbs on the windowsills and clean them off with a chicken feather to symbolically make the house pesachdich (kosher for passover). There was a special set of dishes and pots and pans used only for Passover. He would bury knives in the ground for a certain period to make them pesachdich. When Papa sharpened a knife, he would always test it on his fingernail. I don't know what he ever saw when he looked at the fingernail.

MY YOUTH

Papa, Rae, Celia, a friend, and David, Vilas Pool, Alstead, NH

Papa saved recipes from the newspaper. There were two Yiddish newspapers, the Forward, which he pronounced "Forwartz", published in Boston, and the Morgan Journal. Papa subscribed to the Morgan Journal, which was mailed from New York city and arrived the next day. We used to get mail delivered twice a day, and all the carriers walked. Papa would cut out the recipes from the food section for all the Jewish dishes and paste them in a scrapbook. He liked to experiment with his cooking.

Mervin Gray, Milton Gray and Mendy, 1934

My cousin Merv remembers Papa's mashed potatoes with two poached eggs on top. For 70 years Merv has been asking breakfast waitresses if they have that dish. He recently found it at an IHOP in Delray Beach.

There was a dairy in Bellows Falls. At Passover, a distinguished rabbi would come up from New York to supervise and ensure that production at the dairy was pesachdich. In the early 30's Papa went and learned from him. Thereafter, the prominent New York rabbi stopped coming. Every year three or four days before Passover, Papa would now go and supervise, although the prominent New York rabbi would still certify the products as if he were there. Papa would return from his work with a large quantity of dairy products and a thick wad of cash, avoiding a paper trail for the rabbi.

The seders were a big deal. Neighbors would attend, and in later years, my sisters Dot and Chips (Celia) came home from nursing school and brought friends. One Passover, at the point in the seder where you pour the cup of wine for the prophet Elijah and open the door, there in the open doorway was a reporter for the Claremont Daily Eagle, who had come to write a story about our seder.

For the holiday of Sukkot, we would build a sukkah outdoors, using one wall of the barn and one wall of the house, and spare doors for the other walls. The milk lady brought us pine branches to make a thick roof. We put in a lamp, running an extension cord from the house. We moved in a table and chairs inside, and we ate meals there for 8 days. Even if it rained, the sukkah stayed dry inside.

We took turns getting the mumps and measles. Some of us even got diphtheria and scarlet fever. Once the whole family was quarantined in the house, and our doctor,

Dr. Sanders, made house calls. We never ever went to the doctor's office.

When I was 11 or 12 I began to sell the Literary Digest news magazine. They would mail me a few dozen copies every week, which I would sell for 10 or 15 cents each. I guess people bought them because they felt sorry for me.

My sister Rose went to campfire girls camp for a few weeks one summer where there was a lake, so she was the only one in the family who learned how to swim. There was no place where the Sugar River in Claremont was swimmable, and there was no pool in town.

Every summer the Grays would arrive in their loaded car to stay for three or four weeks. Uncle Abe would drive up with my Aunt Fannie, Aunt Lena and my cousins Merv and Milton Gray, and sometimes their older brother Bob and Lena's husband Dave. Abe and Dave would go back to Dorchester, Massachusetts the next day. The aunts would do all the cooking, and we ate great. We kids would sleep three in a bed, and some would sleep on the floor.

Once a summer, Papa rented a limousine that could hold 11 or 12 people. He never owned a car. The aunts packed a great picnic lunch, Rose made lemon meringue pies, and we travelled to Vilas Pool for the day, a small lake in Alstead, New Hampshire, about 20 miles away. We left at 8 a.m. We sat 4 or 5 across the limo seats, and there were little seats in the back. There is a photo of me, Merv and Milt at the lake. Vilas Pool had swimming, boats, a playground, a ball field, picnic area, and carillon bells that played every hour. We returned home in the evening. That was our one outing every summer.

Aunt Lena and Aunt Fannie

Then our time together in Claremont would be over, and Uncle Abe would return in the car to take them home.

Only I would ride back to Dorchester with them for a few weeks and continue the wonderful time together. They had some neighbor kids our same age. We were 3 boys and 3 girls, and we made quite a crew. We went to Franklin Park, where there was a zoo, an amusement park, and a golf course. The golf course had been built by the WPA, and it still exists. Area and state golf tournaments are held there. We also went to Franklin Field, which had national track meets, lawn bowling, tennis, and other games. Bob Gray was a top-ranked local tennis player and was always seeded in the tournaments played there. Once when he came to Claremont, Bob brought tennis rackets for Rose and me.

We went to Fenway Park four or five times a week by train and subway. We would take corned beef sandwiches on kaiser rolls and pay five or ten cents to sit in the center field bleachers among what they called the Knothole Gang. The Red Sox were a losing team in those years, but we idolized the players. The Sox owner Tom Yawkey kept buying stars from the Philadelphia A's like Lefty Grove, Jimmy Foxx, Joe Cronin, and Rudy York, but it wasn't enough to make them win. I saw Babe Ruth and Lou Gehrig play when the Yankees came to town. On days that we didn't go to the games, we would listen to them on the radio. The announcer, Fred Hoey, was an institution there, one of a kind. They didn't realize he was always drunk until he showed up sober one day.

Later Milt worked as a vendor for several years and would smuggle me into the grandstand, so I didn't have to sit in the bleachers. For a doubleheader, Milt could make $25 in a day. When they took roll call of the vendors, I would hide in the men's room, then come out when it was over. One day I was discovered there, and they escorted me to the bleachers. It was 95 degrees out that day. Milt usually got to sell ice cream, but that day, as a reprisal for smuggling me in, they gave him hot coffee to sell. He didn't make much money that day.

Walking into Fenway for a night game for the first time, you can't believe how beautiful it is, with the perfect green grass. In those days, there was a slope in front of the Green Monster. When there were sellouts, fans also stood right on the field, behind a rope, in front of the outfield fence. If a ball was hit into those fans, it was a ground rule double. The players also left their gloves out on the field when they ran to the dugout at the end of the half inning. The infielders would just flip their gloves onto the edge of the outfield grass. Years later they started taking the gloves back to the dugout with them because players were tripping on them.

We would go on tours downtown to the Boston Herald's offices. Boston had seven newspapers then, five in the morning and two in the afternoon-evening. I read the great Herald sportswriters, like Arthur Sampson and Burt Whitman. The first afternoon edition of a newspaper might post the first two innings of the Red Sox games. Then an hour later, the next edition might have the score after four innings, then six. The rest of the paper usually remained the same.

We would go to the Museum of Natural History, the Museum of Fine Arts, and to vaudeville shows for 10 cents.

We saw all the big names, including Bob Hope when he was just starting out.

Every Sunday Aunt Fannie would make a huge picnic lunch, and we would all load into Uncle Abe's car, a Nash, and go to Nantasket beach on the South Shore. We would go through the small town of Wollaston and stop for ice cream at a small shack, where the owner, Howard Johnson, dished out the ice cream himself. He later created the ice cream, restaurant and motel empire that he gave his name to.

I went to Dorchester each summer until I was 15, when we already started having dates with the girls.

My younger brother David was five or six years younger than me, and I was protective of him. He followed in my footsteps and played all sports. His baseball team was the Detroit Tigers because he liked Hank Greenberg, one of the few Jewish players. Once when I knew the Tigers had the day off, I bet him 5 cents that the Tigers wouldn't win that day. Of course they weren't playing, so they didn't win. I collected the nickel from him. I wonder now how he had gotten a nickel. My allowance was 15 cents a week: ten cents to go to the movies, and five cents for ice cream. I would go to the drugstore every morning to buy the Boston Herald for Papa and me for two cents. Years later, as the Herald drifted conservative, I stopped buying it.

My older sister Rose was the one in charge in the house. Once out on the lawn after supper, we were tumbling, and she broke her left wrist. It did not heal properly, and a few years later, she went to Boston, and they operated on it to fix it.

MY YOUTH

David, Celia, Mendy, Dorothy, Rae, Papa (sitting)

In junior high and high school, I was known to all my friends as "Blumie." In junior high all the boys took "Manual Training". I built a magazine rack, a bookcase with three shelves, and a table lamp. The wooden lamp had a hole drilled through for the wire to the bulb on top. I recently noticed that the lamp I now have on my night table 75 years later is an exact duplicate of the one I had made, only half the height. I didn't realize that until recently. The girls all took Home Economics. They had a kitchen in the school basement, and the kids who couldn't walk home at lunch time had lunch down there. In Junior High and High School, we always walked home for a big lunch which always started with soup.

We had a study hall for an hour every day, so I would do all my homework then so I didn't have to take it home. When we had vacation, I would do my homework on the last day. I have always been a world-class procrastinator. There were 4 courses of study. I took the classical course which prepared us for college with English, history, Latin and French. The French would come in handy later in Algeria, when I would be able to converse with the civilians. There was also the English/scientific course with lots of math and science, which were my bugaboos. There were also the Commercial course of study and the Home Economics course, which were taken mostly by the girls.

Two of my best friends were Ludwig Rozinski, from a Polish family, and Alec Lesnevsky, from a Russian family. Ludwig had a big family with older brothers who were good athletes. The oldest one, Frank, was an All-American small college football center at the University of New Hampshire. He weighed 180. We hung out together at their houses. Their mothers loved me.

We went to all the school athletic games, and to the ice cream parlor, but none of us in the family ever went to a prom. It cost too much. I had bought a turntable for records, 45 rpm, and we could buy records for 15 or 20 cents. In the summer lots of kids would come to our house, and we would dance to the music all night. We danced in the empty dining room/living room area of the house, outside the swinging doors to the shul. With one of the girls from the big Cleary family as my partner, I became a proficient jitterbugger.

I was really the only one in the family who liked to listen to the radio. I would listen to football games, the Penn Relays, and the Kentucky Derby. There was a radio program which had you predict the Dartmouth football scores. Dartmouth was a football powerhouse in those days. I sent in a score prediction, and I won. The prize was free tickets to the next game. We hitchhiked up to Hanover to see it. I sent in another guess the next week, and I won again.

We would go to the movies on Saturdays for ten cents. I liked Westerns and musicals. Ken Maynard in Westerns, and Bing Crosby in musicals were two of my favorites. I like to watch them today on Turner Movie Classics on TV, especially the musicals.

I would sit at night and listen to the Big Bands on the radio performing live at hotels and resorts. There was a Big Band circuit in the '30's: they would play in Boston, then travel to play in Burlington, Vermont. Since Claremont was about halfway between the two, their buses would stop overnight in Claremont, usually on Thursdays in the summer.

All the big-name bands passed through. They would stay at the Hotel Moody, and they would play Thursday nights at the Roseland Ballroom.

The Roseland Ballroom was several miles outside Claremont. It was a huge rustic barn that could hold 1,000 dancing couples. Its walls were half wood and half screen, for ventilation. A dozen times a summer I would hitchhike out to the Roseland, sit down on the grass outside its walls, and listen to the music which poured out through the screens. Those were magical evenings. I got to hear all the Immortals there: Paul Whiteman, with Bing Crosby who was one of his four Rhythm Boys; Benny Goodman, the clarinet player, who played the Lucky Strike Hit Parade on the radio every Saturday night; Glenn Miller, who later died in a plane crash during the war. There was Artie Shaw; the Dorsey Brothers — Jimmy and Tommy; Claude Thornhill; Eddie Duchin, who married a rich society girl who died young; and Buddy Clark, a Dorchester boy who became a star. Everyone in the Grays' neighborhood in Dorchester knew him.

Rudy Vallee was the biggest star, even bigger than Frank Sinatra ever was. He would stay at the hotel while his band went to Roseland to start the show. Around 10 p.m. he would leave the hotel in an open cabriolet convertible, with him sitting up on top of the back seat. People lined the streets to see him as they slowly drove to Roseland. He would join his band for two or three songs, but then he was done, and he would drive back to the hotel, while the band continued the performance without him.

MY YOUTH

Mendy, 1937

On Friday mornings I went to the hotel to see the Immortals as they walked by to get on their buses. I would gape. They have made movies about most of them, and I've seen them all in recent years on the Turner Classic Movies network.

We got report cards six times a year. Papa just assumed that we would all be on the honor roll, and I always was. My Stevens High School class of 1937 was an outstanding class. We started with 125 students, and 123 graduated. Stevens High had the nation's first high school alumni association, dating back to the 1870's. There is an annual reunion for every graduating class, complete with parade and bands. It is the biggest annual event in Claremont, including a banquet which hundreds attend. The Class of '37 was the mainstay of the alumni association for many years.

Lud, Les (Alec) and I celebrated our high school graduation by climbing Mt. Ascutney. They had built a road to the top and trails for the ski resort there. We climbed one of the trails and at the top we ate the lunch we had brought. Then we ran home down the road. The picture of me on the family reunion DVD was taken that day on top of Mt. Ascutney.

I had worked in the office of the Kimmel Shoe factory during school vacations. I was the only male working in the office. My salary was $8.00 a week. I kept $1.00, and I gave Papa $7.00. After I graduated I worked there full time for two years. I made $15.00 a week, which was paid out in cash in an envelope. My friend Alec went to work at GE in Schenectedy, then moved out to Ft. Wayne, Indiana, and I went out to see him after the war. Ludwig went to work in

MY YOUTH

the machine shop of Joy Manufacturing, Claremont's largest employer, making mining drills.

Lud, Mendy, Alec 1937

UNCLE MENDY

In 1939 I went to live in Boston. Abe and Fannie Gray rented an apartment on Gleason St. in Dorchester. Their

Rose, Dorothy, Merv and Mendy

landlord lived above them in the building, and he owned a leather business. He bought leather from tanneries and sold it to the shoe factories. My cousin Merv had worked in the shipping department there for a year, but then he got a different job at Massachusetts Knitting Mills. He told me about the open position, so I came and took his place. I slept on a cot in their apartment, and we lived close to the poverty level. We used to huddle around the kitchen oven for heat in the winter, since the rest of the apartment had no heat. Through 1939 and 1940, I worked for $18 a week, but I gave most of it to Aunt Fannie.

Mendy and David

I spent much of my free time at the Hecht House in Dorchester. It had a gym, and there were clubs and sports teams. There was a Hecht House basketball team, mainly guys in their 20's, and the coach picked me to join their team. I remember on a Saturday night travelling to play in Portland, Maine, 100 miles away, in a car with no heat. We lost. I was cold a lot in those years.

In 1941, my cousin Bob Gray had graduated from the Bentley School of Accounting and Finance, which is now Bentley University. At that time it was just the second floor of one office building. My cousin Mil and I decided that we would enroll there too. In September, we started, attending three or four nights a week in the evening after work. We did our homework together sitting in the kitchen. I was also still playing for my club basketball team, and we were having a perfect season, 0 - 14.

But then my draft number was called, one of the earliest to be chosen. After just five weeks of school, I had to report for active duty in the Army. I had just turned 22 years old.

2

The War Years

I WAS INDUCTED into the U.S. army at Ft. Devens, Massachusetts on October 14, 1941. In a few weeks I was sent to Ft. Belvoir, Virginia for infantry training and engineering training. On Saturday, December 6, I went into Washington, DC with my buddy Jim Theophilis and stayed overnight. Jim had been a sophomore at Wesleyan, and his dad owned a restaurant in Litchfield, Connecticut. We ate that night at a Hungarian restaurant, and I have had a fondness for goulash ever since. On Sunday, Dec. 7, we went to a movie theater and had just finished some popcorn in the lobby before the movie when a lady came up to us and took our hands. "Oh, you poor boys," she said and started crying. We found out that Pearl Harbor had been bombed, and we returned to base without seeing the movie.

The next day, we were all gathered outside in an amphitheater and listened to the radio broadcast of President Franklin Roosevelt's speech declaring war on Japan. After finishing basic training in mid-December, I was sent to Westover Air Base in Chicopee, Massachusetts, where we formed the 809th Combat Engineers Battalion. I was a

UNCLE MENDY

Mendy, 1941

private in the Second Platoon of Company B of the 809th. Our mission was to protect Westover from attack and to train. My buddy Jim went to the 1st Infantry Division at Ft. Bragg. All through January we froze and dug gun emplacements in the frozen ground. Four guys worked together, two with picks and two with shovels. The ground was so hard it took 20 minutes for the two with the picks to dig up one shovelful of earth. We took long marches up by Mt. Holyoke College. For recreation, I played on the Company B basketball team.

In March, 1942, we went to Ft. Dix, New Jersey, where we were sequestered to await embarkation. No phone calls or letters were allowed, as our voyage to England was a secret. In April, we were shipped out aboard the Queen Mary. The cruise ship was filled with 15,000 men, who slept in hammocks. It took four days travelling at a speed of 40 knots, the unescorted ship zigzagging to avoid attack by U-boat submarines. I was seasick the entire time. We landed at Greenock, near Glasgow, Scotland. We were then stationed near Coventry, England, near the Glatton Air Base.

We trained for the invasion of North Africa, and there were German air raids every night. Half of the time we went into bomb shelters, but the other half of the time we did not bother, figuring they would miss us. Guys would pick up pieces of aluminum from the bombs and make rings out of them. The city of Coventry was completely devastated.

I was still known as "Blumie" then, though at roll call I just yelled out my serial number, "31036457!" They would pick one guy from each platoon to get a weekend pass, and once I got one. A buddy from another platoon and I went to London and did some sightseeing. We met a couple of girls, and my friend, who didn't know me that well, introduced me to them as "Mike." The name Mike stuck and seemed simpler, so from then on I became Mike to everyone outside my family. Our British hosts used to say that the problem with the Americans was that we were "overpaid, overfed, oversexed, and over here." While in England, I got an invitation to my sister Rose's wedding to one Ralph Schwartz, whom I had never heard of.

While you were in the U.S., army pay was $21 per month in 1941. Out of that they deducted money to pay for things like laundry, dry cleaning, and life insurance. When I went overseas in 1942, the pay went up to $50 per month, plus an extra $10 for overseas pay. Out of that they deducted money for my allotment of $50 or $55, which was sent home. After the war, my allotments that I had saved and my poker winnings paid for my new car.

Rose and Ralph Schwartz, 1942

In November, we boarded a converted cruise ship which held 10,000 to 15,000 men. It was part of an enormous fleet which sailed from England, and it was smooth sailing into the Mediterranean Sea. On November 8, 1942 we landed at Oran, Algeria. Winston Churchill had been wise not to attempt the invasion of France immediately, but rather to begin with North Africa. It let the inexperienced U.S. military learn from their own bungling. All of our food had been loaded into the ships first — they did not realize that meant it would then be the last thing out when the ships were unloaded. It took them three days to unload the ships. For three days we had nothing to eat, only the oranges which we could pick off the trees.

"My First Vehicle," N. Africa, 1942

We fought our way east across the desert from Algeria to Tunisia. I was a member of a 3-man team that manned a .50 caliber machine gun. A corporal acted as spotter, another private was the feeder of the ammunition belts, and I was the gunner. The machine gun could be mounted on a half-track armored personnel carrier, or on the ground. We slept in a large foxhole we would dig to emplace the machine gun on its tripod. It was winter, and at night it was so cold, two of us would sleep covered with all of our blankets, while the third man who was up on watch would wear all the rest of everyone's spare clothing.

"27-day beard finally removed", N. Africa, 1942

Throughout the entire war, we only knew what was going on in the war in an area of maybe 100 yards around us. One day I saw some guys who wore the patch of the 1st Infantry Division. I asked about my buddy Jim Theophilos from basic training, the one who I'd been in the movie theater with. They told me he'd been killed. Later in life I got interested in reading books about the war to find out what had really gone on. So forty years later I read about the battle of Kasserine Pass and learned that his unit, the 19th Combat Engineers of the 1st Division, had been the ones ordered to hold the pass and had been completely wiped out by General Rommel's troops.

I remember one time we were walking along a road, and I took a pair of binoculars from a dead German soldier. It has numbered axes engraved on the lenses for artillery aiming purposes. His name is etched on them: M.D. Fiedler. I had to hide them throughout the rest of the war during all the inspections, but I got them home. My stomach must have shrunk during the war. We ate C rations, which came in small 8-ounce cans. You carried nine cans in your pack. They were things like stew, hash, and beans. Later we ate K rations, dried food which was lighter to carry. They came in a waxed box 8 inches by 3 inches by 1 inch. They contained a couple of crackers, corned beef, spam, and hard round candies.

Every few weeks when we went to the rear for a couple of days there was a trailer set up by the mess unit, and we got hot meals, cooked in big 10-gallon pots. The mess sergeant was also a baker in civilian life. We would then be able to take a shower. The supply sergeant would issue any new clothes we needed — a lot of clothes were lost or discarded so you wouldn't have to carry them, or too dirty or torn to keep or wash. The mess unit, supply unit and headquarters company worked out of

"Disgusted in N. Africa mud," April, 1942

trailers. When we were not at the front we slept in pyramidal tents, eight men to a tent.

Mendy, N. Africa 1943

In May, 1943, we finally trapped the Germans on a peninsula near Tunis. They surrendered, and the battle for North Africa was over. We captured over 300,000 German prisoners, who were sent back to the U.S. to prison camps or to work at military bases.

"Training for Sicily", 1943 (Mendy with sunglasses)

We camped and trained on the beach near Bizerte for the invasion of Sicily. Once I remember walking with Pete and Joe Alberski several miles along the beach to a town in Tunisia to get some vino, with my legs feeling like lead from walking in the sand. I could barely lift them. One morning I woke up stiff as a board from sleeping on the ground — they had to carry me to sick call on a stretcher. This is where my back problems began.

One day I went into Tunis, and a boy came up with a puppy and asked if I wanted to buy him. I bought him for fifty cents. I named him Tuffy. He kept me warm at night. I actually brought him along in the invasion of Sicily, stored in with the equipment. I had him for 5 months, then had to give him away to a supply sergeant to be taken care of. He was our mascot.

Mendy with Tuffy, June, 1943

We were in tremendous physical shape. I have a photo of some of us playing cards there, with our shirts off, tanned and blackened, wearing our helmet liners.

In early July, 1943, I boarded an LCI (Landing Craft Infantry) and crossed the Mediterranean Sea. We were dumped into waist-high water and waded ashore onto the beaches at Gela, Sicily. I was wounded in the hand by shrapnel, but I just bandaged it and kept on going. I didn't want to go to the hospital and leave my unit. The wound swelled with pus, and months later the piece of shrapnel fell out. At that time you were not awarded the Purple Heart unless you went to the hospital, so I never got my medal. Nowadays they give away Purple Hearts even for accidental self-inflicted injuries.

"Loading LCI for Sicily," July 9, 1943

Due to a mix-up during the invasion, the Navy mistakenly shot down 19 of our own planes filled with 82nd Airborne Division paratroopers. The Navy hadn't been told they were coming. I always resented that the military never admitted to this mistake until 1960. That's why I don't believe much of what the military top brass ever tell us.

"Visiting Sicily," 1943

North of Gela we were set up with our machine gun on a hill, while the company was encamped down below. Two German planes, Messerschmidts, spotted us and dove down making strafing runs over the company with machine gun fire. I began firing at them. Every tenth bullet was a tracer, which burns and allows you to see the trajectory of your firing. When the pilots noticed us, they made two passes over us, shooting to knock us out. On the next pass I was able to lead one just right, and I hit it, and it spiraled down and crashed. The other plane then took off and left us alone.

"Touring Sicily," 1943

"Medal Day, Sicily," 1943 (Pete Caputi on right)

After a month of fighting, the battle for Sicily was over. The Germans retreated to the mainland of Italy. A number of guys who had been wounded had gone back to hospitals in North Africa, and then returned to our unit. Georgie Mollo came back after a few weeks and told us he had been in a hospital tent when General Patton entered and was making the rounds. Georgie witnessed the famous incident where Patton slapped a young soldier, accusing him of malingering, which resulted in Patton being reprimanded by General Eisenhower.

In September, 1943, we invaded the mainland of Italy on the beaches at Salerno. While on the beachhead, a shell landed too close to me, causing a total hearing loss in my left ear.

Italy, 1943

Our mission was to move north through Italy to take Rome. Our unit freelanced throughout the war and was moved around to where we were most needed. We were not part of any division, but were attached to some, mostly to the 3rd, 34th, 35th, and 45th Infantry Divisions. The 809th became famous and was celebrated for its achievements. We did a multitude of different things: we were engineers, we were infantry, we went out on patrols. My red scarf comes from when we were attached to the 34th Infantry Division; they were from Texas and the red scarf with a steer on it was their emblem.

My highest rank was corporal, but as casualties mounted, they would transfer experienced noncoms around to be cadre for other units loaded with replacements. They were going to transfer me as a corporal, so in order to stay with my unit at one point, I had to accept becoming a private again. But I was proud to be a first-class private.

In Italy the terrain was mountainous, and the weather was cold, wet and miserable. The German soldiers put up a tough defense. Winter blizzards began in December. It was the coldest winter they had had there in many years. We bogged down, and the advance was very slow. There were many casualties. Sometimes in a whole week we had not been able to move forward more than a few yards.

Italy, 1943

A lot of what happened is pretty hazy in my memory now. We were young, and to protect ourselves, we didn't allow ourselves to dwell on what was happening. Maybe in order to get through it, we refused to let it form a lasting impression on us. I really enjoyed the comradeship. But we didn't get too close with the replacements who joined us, because they often didn't last very long. Survival was a matter of experience and luck. What helped me was that I never took it seriously. I never worried that I would get shot the next day. My attitude was that whatever was going to happen would happen. Now, I think that shows stupidity, but it worked.

There's a saying that, "There are no atheists in a foxhole." I never believed that. When you're in that foxhole, with the shells flying, you realize that there can't possibly be a God, or this wouldn't be happening. My observation was that praying didn't help.

The fighting at the Rapido River and at Monte Cassino was the worst I was in. In one attack we put up a pontoon bridge halfway across the Rapido River under heavy fire which was then swept away, dumping many guys into the water, who drowned. In all the documentaries that I've seen of the war, the film of that incident is the only film I've seen of the exact spot where I was at the time.

The generals knew it was hopeless but threw us into it. They would have brainstorms and would send us forward to do things to prove they were doing something, which ended in disasters. They knew that whatever we did was usually doomed, resulting in many unnecessary deaths.

In January, 1944, the battle for the mountaintop monastery of Monte Cassino began. Cassino guarded the only road north, heavily defended by the Germans, who were dug in. They were a couple of thousand feet above us on the mountain. We were down below like sitting ducks. After a month of heavy fighting, on February 15, our airplanes finally bombed the monastery and leveled it. But even that was no help to us — it only gave the Germans better hiding places.

"Washing off weeks of grime," Avellino, Italy, 1943

We fought together with troops from Great Britain, France, Canada, India, Australia, New Zealand, and the Goums, who were Moroccan natives who carried machetes and never took a prisoner. It took us another full three months of fighting to capture that mountain, and we slept in foxholes the whole time. That was when I swore that I would never be cold again. The parka I wore is still in my closet, camouflaged white on one side, olive drab on the other.

I recently read a book about the battle for Monte Cassino, and I found out it was a lot worse than I had even thought.

Every three or four weeks, we could go into Naples for a day or two. We went to the Red Cross, whose people stayed in the best hotels there. They had the nerve to charge us 10 or 15 cents for coffee and a donut. Consequently, I do not have a love for the Red Cross.

Our only contact with home was the V-mail. Sometimes there were long periods when we got no mail, and we were not able to send any home. Once my sister Dorothy mailed me a loaf of bread she had baked. After six weeks in transit, it felt hard as a rock, but it was unusually heavy, so I knew there must be something inside it. I had to use a rifle butt to break it open. It turned out to be a bottle of Johnny Walker scotch that she had hidden inside it.

After taking Cassino, General Mark Clark wanted to be the first to get to Rome. He was racing the British, and he must have had ten public relations guys working for him. We liberated Rome on June 5, 1944. But we were relegated to the back pages of the newspapers the next day, which happened to be June 6, D-Day, the invasion of France. We resented the fact that the guys in France got all the press attention after that.

We continued on to Florence. Then in July, we were pulled out for the invasion of southern France, my fourth invasion. The advance in Normandy had been stymied, so the generals felt that a second front in southern France would help out. The 809th went there to take part in the landings, and we moved up the Rhone Valley for a few weeks. General Patton commanded a few divisions that continued on into northern France. But we were returned to Italy and put back in the front lines. As we went through one town after another, the Italians cheered and waved flags and handed us bottles of wine. They kept their girls hidden from us though.

I got a weekend pass to Rome, and I stayed in the complex that Mussolini had built for the Olympics which didn't take place. Then they were giving us one or two-week leaves, and some of the guys were traveling as far as England. I was planning on hitchhiking to France to try to find my brother David's unit. But in August I got a three-page letter from Rose's husband Ralph, giving me the bad news that David had been killed in Normandy.

"On leave with Thaddeus Lynch," Rome, 1944

We were in Bologna when the war ended in May, 1945. There was a point system in order to get sent home. You got points for each month of active service, each month overseas, for invasions, for campaigns. When you accumulated 85 points, you were eligible to be shipped home and reassigned or discharged.

My Record:

Points

45	Service - 45 months (1 point per month)
36	Overseas - 36 months (1 point per month)
40	Campaigns - 8 (5 points each)
20	Invasions - 4 (5 points each)
141	Total points

141 points was probably the most of any unit in the European-Mediterranean theatre.

"Heading Home," Italy, April 1945

Three of us were among the first to be sent to Naples for reassignment — Tom McGlone, Ted Lynch, and myself. They were sending most of the guys to the Pacific, where the war was still going on. The replacement depot officer behind the table there looked over our papers and our record in 8 campaigns: Algeria-French Morocco; Tunisia; Sicily; Salerno-Naples-Foggia; Cassino-Rome-Arno; Southern France; North Apennines; Po Valley.

He looked up at us and asked incredulously, "What are you guys still doing here?" He sent us home for discharge.

We left Naples in May, 1945 on a Liberty ship and arrived in Newport News, Virginia two weeks later. I was seasick the entire time and lost 30 pounds, down to 140.

On our first morning back in the U.S., a sergeant came into the barracks and woke us up to go outside for reveille and some close-order drill. You never saw a man fly back out the door and down the steps so fast in your life. We almost killed the guy. We were grizzled veterans. Nobody bothered us again.

The first time in the chow line back home seemed like paradise. In the mess hall, captured German prisoners were serving the food as you went down the line with your tray. They saw our 5th Army patches and started pointing and talking among themselves. It turns out they were prisoners whom we had captured in North Africa, and they had spent the rest of the war working in the mess hall in the comfort of Virginia. They couldn't thank us enough. They piled the food high on our trays and kept giving us more. That night I got sick and threw it all up.

A couple of days later we were put on a train north for Ft. Devens, Massachusetts, that had an old coal-burning locomotive. It took us two days to get to Providence. By that time we were unshaven and covered with black soot from the coal smoke that blew in the open windows on us. When the train stopped for a few hours in Providence, we went across the street from the station to the Biltmore Hotel. We were looking as scraggly as Joe and Willy, the GI characters in the famous newspaper cartoons of Bill Mauldin. We stepped into the bar which was packed with well-dressed people having lunch. They all looked up at us, and an absolute silence fell over the room. Then suddenly there was a lot of noise and commotion as people were coming over to congratulate us, and the free drinks just didn't stop flowing. We stumbled back to the train just in time before it left.

We were at Ft. Devens for about two weeks being processed. I regained the weight I'd lost coming home in the Liberty ship. While there I went to Boston to my Aunt Fannie's apartment, and she was there with my Aunt Lena, my sister Rose, and Dave Grodensky, Lena's husband. Lena looked me over and then said with wonderment, "He looks exactly the same as he did when he left!"

We were discharged at Ft. Devens in June, 1945.

I took the train to Claremont, and my sister Rae met me at the junction with a neighbor's car and drove me home. I saw on the front window of the house there were two blue stars, for family members serving in the military, myself and Chips, and the one gold star, for my brother David who had been killed in France. My father was standing behind the counter in the barn. "Hi, Papa," I said. We hugged each other and cried a little.

UNCLE MENDY

Medals and gravestone of David Blumberg

Mendy's medals

World War II Memorial, detail, Washington, D.C.

3
From Claremont to Florida

THE DAY AFTER I got back, I put on my uniform and walked down Pleasant Street, the main street in Claremont, for the first time in seven years. I stopped into stores, and said hello to people I knew. In Heller's clothing store, I had a very emotional reunion with the guys I knew. When I got home, I looked in our closet and found some of David's clothes, which fit me. After a few days, I bought some clothes and shoes at Heller's.

I took a few months off to travel around starting in July. First I went to Boston by train and visited the Grays, and stayed with Aunt Lena. Then I travelled to Newport, Rhode Island to see Milt, who was stationed there in the Navy. Then I took the train to New York City to see Merv, who met me at Grand Central Station. Merv was also in the Navy, in Brooklyn. It happened to be the day, July 28, that a B-25 bomber had crashed in fog into the Empire State Building. We went by there and looked up at the rear half of the plane, which was sticking out of the side of the building. I stayed in Merv's apartment for a while. Then I took the train to Chicago to visit Rose and meet Ralph. Martha was just a few months old, and Rae was also visiting them. I stayed a few days in another apartment in their building. Ralph got me tickets to Comiskey Park to see the White Sox play the Red Sox.

Mendy and Mervin, 1945

Then I took the train to Ft. Wayne, Indiana to see Alec, who was working for GE. On the train, I heard the news on a portable radio that Japan had surrendered, ending World War II. Alec was living in a virtual frat house there. A few days later, I took the train back to Claremont.

I went into Heller's clothing store, and Sam Heller asked

me if I wanted to go to work there. Rae had gone back to school, and Papa was alone, so I took Sam up on his offer. My job was calculating the prices which could be charged for items: in those days prices were fixed, with the government establishing what the maximum rate of profit could be. In addition, I was a salesman. We sold all the best brands: Hart, Schafner & Marks, Arrow shirts, Florsheim shoes. It was a fine store, where many on the Dartmouth faculty bought their clothes. When a salesman assisted new customers, from then on those customers would ask for that salesman whenever they came into the store. I developed a lot of regular customers. I made them laugh, and they looked forward to my humor. We were very busy, especially at Christmas.

I would go to Sam with suggestions. Most of the time he would say, "That makes sense," and follow my suggestions, though sometimes he did not. Mrs. Hutcheon worked in the tailor shop. She told me great Scottish jokes. She had lost her only child, Edwin, in the war. I can only imagine how devastating it was for her. She kind of adopted me, maybe substituting me for her lost son. We had a loving relationship, and I made her feel better.

Abe Heller gave me driving lessons in the store's pickup truck. They would call the Concord store to see if they had items in stock, and I would drive the truck 50 miles for practice with Abe in the passenger seat. I took my driver's test with the pickup truck and passed. Abe was the youngest of the four Heller boys and two girls. He was only five feet tall. He must have been one of the first two-handed swinging tennis players. He left Claremont in 1946 to get some hormone treatment, which allowed him to grow, and he later become a well-known psychologist. I took over Abe's duties when he left. Every morning I would go over the shipment of clothes that had come in and calculate what the prices should be under the government price guidelines. There was a big government book which told you how much you could mark things up. I would make the price tags and put them on the items. When I was done, I would go out on the floor as a salesman. My training at Heller's formed the desire I have had for the rest of my life to be impeccably dressed.

At that time cars were being rationed to the car dealers, as the factories were still changing over from making military vehicles. A car salesman, Ed Cleary, lived across the street from us, and they were getting only 8 new cars in the year, but he had told me I was at the head of the list, as returning servicemen got preference. In September, 1945, he called to say my car was there, and it would cost $1,300.

During the war, I was paid $60 a month: basic pay of $50, and an extra $10 for serving overseas. I had $50 of it sent home as an allotment, so I had money saved. I went to the bank to make a withdrawal and asked for one $1,000 bill, and three $100 bills. At work I called over Morris, the presser in the tailor shop, and showed him the $1,000 bill. When his eyes popped back in his head, he asked if he could borrow it for a few minutes. He took it next door, ordered a cup of coffee, and tried to pay for it with that bill. That caused a sensation, and then he paid with a $1 bill.

My new car was a two-door two-tone Chevy Deluxe,

with a dark blue roof and a light blue body. I drove it home and tooted the horn for Papa to come out. He admired it, and then I gave him a ride around the block. Later on I drove him up Mt. Ascutney once, just so he could see and feel what it was like at the top there. I used the barn as a garage, as the car fit perfectly onto our basketball court. I drove to work until winter came, when I would leave the car in the barn and walk to work. In those days to drive in snow you would put metal chains around the rear tires. You would hear all the cars clanking their chains as they drove in winter.

First car, Claremont, 1946

I led an active social life. I got together with a few of my National Guard friends, and we would take dates to the Roseland, and to Newport, New Hampshire. With my discount at Heller's, I built up quite a wardrobe of suits and sport coats. I wore suspenders and had three or four pairs of shoes.

Mendy, Claremont, 1946

My dancing partner at Roseland was Dorothy Loudon, who had been a classmate of Rae's in high school. She had gone to college at Syracuse. She eventually went to New York City, where she sang at supper clubs and became a well-known chanteuse. She was a leading cabaret singer, acted in numerous films and shows, and she won a Tony award for "Annie" in the 1970's. I looked her up on the Internet and found that somewhere along the way she had lost six or seven years. She and Rae would have had to graduate at age 11.

In the spring of 1946 I got two season tickets at Fenway Park, in the 17th row between home plate and the Red Sox dugout. It was a weekend and holiday package that cost me about $70. I instantly became very popular. I would arrange to get Saturdays off from work, and I would drive the four hours to Boston for the games and stay over at the Kenmore Hotel, which was around the corner from Fenway Park. My friends would pay for the gas and hotel in exchange for their ticket.

I hung around with two guys in the New Hampshire National Guard who had served a year in 1940, then had been called back in 1941. We met two girls who were counselors at a camp at Lake Sunapee, and one of them became the first romance of my life. Thus began a wonderful summer. I took her to the games at Fenway. She was in college and lived in Belmont, near Boston. That summer I did lots of travelling and not much sleeping. But I was actually saving up money, earning $50 a week plus a substantial Christmas bonus. With our employee discounts, I built up a great wardrobe.

When camp ended, she went back to school. She would cut class, and we would go to the ballgame. The Red Sox won the pennant that year by 15 or 20 games. Back then there were no baseball playoffs, just the World Series, and my tickets were not good for the Series.

Rose's husband Ralph owned the dry cleaning concession at the Ritz Carlton Hotel. A customer who was a politician gave Ralph a ticket to game six of the World Series. Knowing what a big Red Sox fan I was, Ralph called and offered me the ticket. Thus I drove to Boston and got to see a World Series game. I hadn't realized that Ralph was giving me his only ticket. It turned out to be a ticket in the Joseph P. Kennedy family box. I recognized Ambassador Joe Kennedy there, the police commissioner of Boston, and a couple of the older Kennedy boys, but I didn't know any of the others. The Red Sox lost, but I saw the famous play where Enos Slaughter of the Cardinals scored all the way from first base on a single for the winning run.

In November, 1946, on the day after Thanksgiving, two feet of snow fell on Claremont. I was looking out the window watching it fall, and I said, "I'm never going to shovel this again." I told Papa I was going to Florida to get warm. I packed all my possessions — which were just my clothes — and drove to New York to pick up my friend Pete Caputi, and we drove to Key West non-stop. We saw a lot of devastation in Florida from a recent hurricane. We just stayed in Key West for a day, then we drove back to Miami Beach and rented a room in a residential hotel near Ocean Drive for $15 a week.

We lived like tourists, me on unemployment, Pete on disability for his wound in the ass. We didn't intend to stay in Florida permanently, but we didn't think ahead at all. We ended up staying four or five months. During the first two months, we would go to the beach and Gulfstream racetrack a lot, but I don't remember too much else, except the delicious food in the cafeterias where it was all you can eat. Then we moved to Miami, to a large boarding house with six bedrooms on N.E. 25th Street. It was one block off Biscayne Boulevard, the wide tree-lined main street which runs north-south and is also U.S 1. Three stewardesses had moved in, and one of them became the second romance of my life. American Airlines used to furlough many of its personnel for the winter and then call them back to work in the spring. There was a third guy in the house besides Pete and me — his name was Pat, and he worked for Eastern Airlines.

We paired off, and there were three romances going on. There was Phyllis, Bernice, and my girlfriend, Dusty. She was called Dusty because her last name was Dostie. She was from Natick, Massachusetts, and had gone to Chamberlain College. She was beautiful, with blonde hair. The six of us were together all the time. I had the only car in the boarding house.

Mendy and Dusty

Around 17th St. there was the S&S Diner. It was annually voted the best place for breakfast or lunch in Miami. It was in the center of the Miami auto dealership area and was very lucrative. It had a U-shaped counter, and chairs around the sides where people waited for a seat at the counter. The owner was a kindly old Greek, Louis Cavalaris, and his whole family worked there. We would walk to breakfast there every day, then go to the beach in south Miami near the University of Miami at Matheson Hammock, an isolated sheltered cove about 100 yards long. We became real friendly with Louis, Sr., who was a real gambler. He owned and stabled a few racehorses at Tropical Park racetrack in west Miami. He had figured it would be easier to win bets if he were on the inside.

His son L.C., Jr. was a short order cook at the restaurant, and he was also the horse trainer. He would go to Tropical to train the horses in the morning, then go back to the diner to work as a cook. If he had a horse running, he would stay at the track for the afternoon. L.C., Jr. did not have a car, so he asked me if we could give him a ride back and forth. Pete and I began helping him to walk the horses at the track, and he soon got us badges which got us admitted to all three tracks: Tropical, Hialeah and Gulfstream. We became so friendly with the Cavalaris family that they began feeding us on the house. We offered to pay, but the old man wouldn't take our money. In return, we would help out around the restaurant, like carry out the garbage cans. If L.C., Jr. had a horse in a race, we would go sit in their box at the track and watch the race, and then we would get in the picture in the winner's circle if we won.

In the evening we would walk to downtown with the girls down Biscayne Boulevard to the restaurants, a beautiful ten to fifteen minute walk. We would eat, then window shop on the way back. This went on for about four months, when the girls were called back to work. Dusty was based in Newark, New Jersey.

In April, the Florida horses went north to race in Chicago, New Jersey, New York, and Boston. Pete and I drove north in the spring of 1947. Pete's parents lived in upper Manhattan. I was staying at my father's apartment on 87th St., living on my unemployment checks and my savings. Dusty was living in a rooming house in Newark. I would take the Pulaski Skyway there, since it was before they had built the New Jersey Turnpike or Garden State Parkway. I would drive Dusty to the airport, and then I would pick her up when her flights came back in. We used to go to a restaurant in the country named the Log Cabin to eat and dance.

This went on for a while. I took Dusty to see her family in Natick. Her mother, a French Canadian Catholic, did not like me, probably because I was unemployed, and maybe because I was Jewish, but we continued our relationship because we were madly in love. But later in 1947 Dusty was transferred to Chicago, and that was that. We were both devastated. Pete meanwhile got a job in New York City on Wall Street.

My father had also moved to New York City. In 1946, the congregation Agudas Achim had bought an abandoned school in Claremont and built Temple Meyer David, named after my friend Meyer Satzow and my brother David. Both of them had been killed in Normandy. Meyer had been a year behind me in high school, and had been in ROTC at the University of New Hampshire. Meyer's family owned a slaughterhouse. Once the two of us picked up some calves in their truck. When we were driving back, the truck skidded on a bridge, and we were only saved from going over the side by a bridge cable. Our house in Claremont, built in the 1800's, is now a historic site with a plaque. The shul has been remodeled into a few rooms.

After the new temple was built in Claremont, my father moved to New York city, to a one-bedroom apartment on the 3rd floor on East 87th Street, in the same building where Rae and Celia lived downstairs. He became employed at a nearby shul, and conducted morning and evening services and acted as a shamos, helping out with the library and other things. He belonged to the Swiechiany Association, an organization in downtown New York comprised of people from his hometown in Lithuania. He learned his way around and went to Levittown and Metuchen on the train to visit Rose and Dorothy.

On Saturday, November 22, 1947, the 809th held its first reunion at the Hotel Commodore in New York City. Since we were mostly a New England, New York and Northeast outfit, 125 guys showed up at the first reunion. Many of the original guys had survived the war. We were carousing together all day. There was only a curtain separating our banquet room from the back of the stage of the theater. The management asked us to keep the noise down, because a young singer from Brooklyn was making his debut there that evening. If we had not complied — which would have been possible, since we were all in our 20's and had been drinking all day — you might never have heard of the young singer who was then able to take the stage that night and become a big success, Vic Damone. That was our first reunion, and we continued to hold them every year on a Saturday. I could not attend for many years, until after I retired. In the mid-1980's, they started being held in the Poconos for a whole weekend.

First Reunion of 809th, New York City, Nov. 22, 1947 (Mendy back row, far right)

UNCLE MENDY

Gray Family   Row 1: Roz, Fannie, Anita, Shirley   Row 2: Merv, Abe, Bob, Milt

4
Life on the Back Stretch

I WENT BACK to Miami alone that fall and got a room near the Orange Bowl, in what is now Little Havana. I remember that winter the Ivy League sent their polo teams down there to play in the Orange Bowl. L.C., Jr. and I resumed our friendship, and I was put on the payroll. I walked the horses, helped groom them and prepared them for races. In the winter, Pete came back to Florida on vacation. At the beach we met a couple from Rockford, Illinois, who owned a prestigious gift shop. We became friendly with them, and they asked Pete if he wanted to go back north with them. He did, and he ended up working and managing in their gift shop for the next 20 or 25 years.

When the Florida racing season was over, L.C., Jr. got stalls at Suffolk Downs in Boston. I went north with him as an assistant trainer and chauffer. We had ten to twelve horses, and we raced them there. I frequently got to see the Grays, who had set up their own accounting firm in downtown Boston, called Gray, Gray & Gray. I saw Rose and Ralph, and would go to Malden and got to know Ralph's family: his parents Nathan and Dora, and his sister Ann and her husband Jack, and his sister Edie and her husband Hal. Hal was a catcher on a baseball team, and we used to go see him play. After eight weeks when racing at Suffolk was done, we continued on the New England circuit, for two months at Rockingham track in Salem, New Hampshire, on the Massachusetts border near Lawrence, Massachusetts and Nashua, Manchester, and Concord, New Hampshire, and then for two months we went to Naragansett Park, near Providence, Rhode Island.

I felt that not everyone in the family approved of what I was doing, but I was doing what I wanted. I made friends, I didn't bet, and most days I would spend the afternoon in the grandstand reading a book and watching the races. In 1949 and 1950, we wintered in Florida and then did the New England circuit again in the spring, summer and fall. L.C., Jr. had a girlfriend in northern Ohio, and someone suggested he go up to the nearby Woodbine track in Toronto, which he did. But I stayed back in the States. L.C., Jr. and I had not just been boss and employee — we were friends.

I met Charlie Huddleston, who was the stable manager for B.B. Williams, a noted trainer with a stable of fifty horses owned by members of high society, like the Whitneys and the Vanderbilts. I joined them, and we raced the New Jersey circuit: Garden State near Philadelphia, Monmouth near Long Branch, and Atlantic City. After the horses were fed at 4:00 p.m., Charlie and I would have a cocktail hour, and sit and talk. He had a large steamer trunk with pull-out drawers installed that served as his bar. He always insisted on Beefeaters gin for his martinis. Once again I freeloaded.

For several more years we raced the New Jersey circuit in the summer and the Florida circuit in the winter: Tropical Park, Hialeah, and Gulfstream. Then I got tired of all the travel, and the packing and unpacking. I returned to Hallandale, Florida, which at that time was a little town of 3,000 people just north of Miami.

While working at Gulfstream I became friendly with the track veterinarian, Dr. Clarence Dee. He had been an all-conference lineman at Iowa State and was so strong, he could wrestle a horse. He had arms like Popeye. In the winter in Florida there were probably 1,000 horses at each of the three tracks, and there were just two vets for all of them. Since Doc Dee lived in Hollywood, which is adjacent to Hallandale to the north, he was most often at Gulfstream. He asked me if I would be interested in working as his assistant. I agreed.

Each morning we traversed the Gulfstream stable area from one end to the other attending to the horses. I prepared medications, kept the records of treatments, kept track of appointments, and in general assisted him with everything. Before long, other trainers and track workers were calling me Doc too. At that time vitamin B-12 injections were popular — it was one of the only medications which was legal then in the 1950's. Many trainers ordered two shots a week, and we would go right down the shed row giving the shots. We would check out any horse that wasn't acting properly. We would give a horse castor oil into its stomach by means of a tube in its nose. A horse's thin legs are normally cold, since they do not have much blood in them. If a leg felt warm, that was a sign that something was wrong.

Doc Dee and I were extremely busy every day. He was also the state's vet, so we checked every horse that would be racing that day. We went from stall to stall in the receiving barn, and if he found something wrong with a horse, he scratched him from the race. There were 10 races with a total of about 80 horses each day. Then after each race, Doc would swab each winner's tongue, and a urine sample would be taken. These were sent off to the lab in Tallahassee to test for prohibited substances.

Hialeah was about 30 minutes away, and Tropical about 45 minutes, and we would drive to those tracks together from Gulfstream when they were racing. We would stop for lunch, and we would go to driving ranges along the way and hit golf balls. I did not know anything about golf then, so I would just go up and hit a bucket of balls. But I was pretty good. Doc Dee was left-handed and crushed the ball.

At the end of each month, I would go to Doc Dee's animal hospital and prepare the bills from the records I had kept. Doc had an animal hospital with his brother-in-law in Hollywood. The next day at the track, I would hand the bills out. In those days the owners paid the vet bills personally. I was friendly with his brother-in-law's son, Tucker Frederickson. During summer vacation, Tucker worked at the animal hospital, and we became quite close. I regaled him with stories of sports in the '30's. Tucker became an All-American running back at Auburn, was the #1 pick in the NFL draft in 1965, and played for the N.Y. Giants for six years.

Doc Dee lived on a farm outside Hollywood that had 10 horse stalls and a large pasture with a track in it. During the season he would collect ailing horses and bring them to his farm, and during the summer off-season he would doctor them. I would take a jockey out to the farm, who would gallop the healing horses as part of their therapy. In the summer, Doc made house calls out in the country on cattle and horses, and I would go with him, keep the records, and do the billing.

I worked with Doc for a few years. It was a very lucrative job. Doc was so busy, he eventually gave up being the vet for the state and having to be at the races 6 days a week. Then he had more of a chance to get out on the golf course.

One day as I was leaving the stable area at Gulfstream, I saw a beautiful woman walking her dog, a boxer. I professed an interest in dogs and introduced myself to her, Louise Farrand. She was living for the winter in a large apartment house with her ailing father, who was a professional gambler. She had accompanied him to Florida to take care of him, but he never left the house. I never saw him, but Louise and I rapidly became friendly, then started dating and being together and going to the beach together.

Every day her father studied the racing form and selected the one best bet that he wanted to make. Each day he would give Louise $400 to $800 to bet, a huge sum in those days, usually on a late race when the better horses ran, and form held up. Most of his choices were favorites and seldom paid more than 2 to 1. Occasionally he wouldn't be able to make a selection and would skip a day. The selection in his mind had to be a sure thing.

I would meet her outside the house, and we would walk through the stable area to the grandstand to place his bet. Most of the time he won, and he made a considerable amount of money.

Louise was a professional dancer. She had been in Broadway shows and on TV. She and her father lived in Hartsdale, New York. When the meet ended, they went back up north, and I went to New York too. She was auditioning for the June Taylor dancers on the Jackie Gleason show. This was an elite group of 16 dancers who began every show, comparable to the Rockettes. She also was a model for bathing suits and bikinis. I would drive her around to her modeling jobs in New York city. I would go up and wait in the photography studio. On weekends we would go up to Connecticut, or to inns along the Hudson.

Louise made the June Taylor dancers, and she became the end girl on the right on TV, the one with black hair and bangs. I would get a ticket to the telecast, then pick her up at the stage door, and we would go out. She got a job at Jones Beach as a dancer in "Kismet." There was an amphitheater with the stage out in the water.

I got a job with Levitt homes that summer. Levitt revolutionized the construction industry by building homes like on an assembly line with specialists just doing one thing in each house. My job was to plaster over the drywall, filling in the cracks and covering the nail heads. I was fast, and since we got paid by the house, I made big money.

Louise had a room in Freeport, and I think I was renting a room with one of Rose's neighbors in Levittown. I remember taking Louise to Rose's once to pick up my bathing suit, and Rae was in the kitchen, and I introduced them to each other. I think that might have been one of the only times that someone in the family met one of my girlfriends.

Rose, Mendy, Dorothy, Celia and Rae

When winter came, I had a yen to return to Florida. I only saw Louise again on television. Some years later the Jackie Gleason show moved to Miami Beach, but by then I was involved with Eleanor. Once I went to a celebrity Pro-Am golf tournament in Miami with my camera, and I went up to Jackie Gleason who was sitting in a golf cart and asked if I could take his picture. His answer was, "Fuck off, kid." In 2008, an article appeared in the Palm Beach Post about Louise and her career. She was now 80 and living in South Palm Beach. She still looked real good.

L.C., Jr. continued to prosper as a horse trainer in Canada. He found a patron in wealthy Peter Fuller, son of a former Massachusetts governor. In 1968, one of my most thrilling moments was to watch the Kentucky Derby on television and see L.C., Jr. and his horse, Dancer's Image, win the Derby. Unfortunately, after the race the horse tested positive for "bute" —phenylbutazone — a common aspirin which was legal everywhere except in Kentucky. It turned out the vet there had a shady past. Both L.C., Jr. and the horse were suspended, and the crown was taken away from them. You can read about the whole story on the Internet. But L.C., Jr. ended up as horse racing commissioner of Canada, and in the Canadian Horse Racing Hall of Fame.

5
A Courier On His Appointed Rounds

WHEN I FIRST moved to my cottage in Hallandale, a small town of 3,000, there was no home mail delivery. Everyone had a post office box. I wanted one with a number that would be easy to remember, like 111 or 222. They told me to look for an empty one, and I found 666. It was 25 years later that I found out that number is associated with the devil.

I became friendly with the postmaster and the several postal employees, and they hired me to help out at Christmas time. At that time they would cancel the outgoing mail and put it into a big canvas bag which would be placed on a hook atop a pole next to the railroad track. When the train went by, it would slow down, and a conductor on the train would lean out with a long pole, hook the canvas bag, and take it into the train and on its way.

In 1962, when they were starting home delivery, they suggested that I go to take the civil service test in Miami. I scored 100 +. They were building the tall condo high-rise buildings at the beach at that time. The other carriers wanted to work closer to their homes, so as the junior employee

I was given the new route at the beach high-rises. It turned out that I had gotten the plushest route: the other carriers used scooters, while I drove a Chevy van there and delivered eventually to 5 buildings, putting the mail in the boxes in the lobby and mail rooms. The Christmas tips were terrific. Each building's board would tip $750 to $1,000, and the individual residents were generous with tips. The guys on the scooters would get a few bucks here and there. Eventually they built a big new post office, and Hallandale grew to a 30,000 population. When I retired at age 62, there was terrific bidding to get my route, and the senior guy got it.

I got to know so many of my customers, who were mostly retirees, and consequently I was very popular. It turns out some of Nardy Certilman's relatives lived in one of my buildings, as well as two aunts of Anita Gray, and a salesman from Abbott Labs who had been friends with Mike Donner. He never did anything with his wife because he had to save his money for the grandchildren. One of the residents was Buster Winick, a friend of Merv and mine from Dorchester. I used to see him often and reminisce about those days.

Before the fifth high-rise condominium building was completed, I covered the small community of Golden Isles, about thirty luxury homes on Hallandale Boulevard en route to the beach. Among my patrons there was Jim Bishop, the author. His popular books were "The Day Lincoln was Shot" and "The Day Kennedy was Shot." We talked to each other every day. He was a famous syndicated columnist, so I would read his column in the morning and see him later in the day. He gave me an autographed copy of "A Day in the Life of JFK."

Another resident there was Meyer Lansky, the famous Jewish gangster. We talked every day about sports and politics. I saw him each morning as he was walking his wife's little white poodle. He was always dressed in a suit and a fedora. He had run the gambling in Havana until Castro took over. To me, he was nothing but a gentleman. Later he moved to a condo in Miami Beach where he had breakfast every morning with his buddies at Wolfie's deli. Then he moved to Israel, saying he wanted to become a citizen and die in Israel, although later Golda Meir kicked him out, presumably because of his reputation. Before he moved, one morning around Christmas, he told me, "I've been looking for you," and he gave me a $100 bill.

A clerk at the post office, Frank DePalma, got me interested in golf. I never had a golf lesson. I read some books, including one by Tommy Armour, and tried to emulate what they described. I had a geometric eye, so I was good at putting. I would go to the Diplomat Hotel par 3 course just down the road and play four or five balls at once to develop my short game. I was deadly from six inches.

Frank and I would arrange for the same day off and go to public courses, meeting before dawn and waiting for them to open. Frank scored in the mid to low 70's. In his youth Frank had worked as a caddy. He won the caddy tournament, and became caddy champ, at his club in Englewood, New Jersey. Members of neighboring clubs would have their caddy champs compete so they could bet on their caddy. Once he played the caddy champ from another club, and he was trounced. Years later he found out that he had lost to golfing great Byron Nelson.

Frank gave me much-needed instruction, and I worked down to a 12 handicap. I returned to the post office one afternoon in November, 1963, and Frank greeted me with, "President Kennedy was shot and killed." I joined the Broward County Golf Association, which held tournaments on weekends at public and private courses. Over time I acquired a number of trophies and a fine golf wardrobe. I enjoyed friendly games as well as competition, as I always played against myself. In Miami the National Association of Letter Carriers, our union, had a golf association, so I kept pretty busy with golf. The National Association had an annual four-day tournament open to all members. In the mid-'60's I arranged the national tournament one year at Ft. St. Lucie. Two hundred players came, as well as wives and girlfriends, and I was in charge of the arrangements. During the first two days I was teamed up with a union vice-president from Washington, D.C. He suggested that I go to work at the main office of the NALC in Washington. I respectfully declined, but I wonder what would have happened had I gone and joined the union hierarchy.

Near my house was a German restaurant, the Hofbrau House. I got friendly with the owners and with one of the waitresses around 1960. Her name was Eleanor. She was divorced and lived in North Miami Beach. Thus began a twenty-year love affair. She was the reason that I did not want to move away to Washington. Eleanor was Italian and originally from Batavia, New York. Her brothers owned a number of pizza parlors up there.

We lived about 15 minutes apart. We both worked from 6:00 a.m. to 3:00 p.m. and then would go to her house. I would stay at her house, but I also maintained my apartment near the post office. In the morning we would go to work, stopping at Dunkin Donuts for our alleged breakfast. Later, she worked at Pumpernick's Deli. One of her customers was Sid Luckman, the great football quarterback.

We led a busy social life. One year we went to Las Vegas for a week and stayed at the Stardust. We saw shows with Wayne Newton, Peggy Lee, and the Folies Bergere. We stopped back in Ft. Lauderdale for the weekend, and then went off to Jamaica for a week at the Playboy Club at Ocho Rios. Most other times we would vacation together in Florida. We liked Naples, a small town on the west coast. Many times in the afternoon on the way to her house I would stop at the county golf course and play a quick nine holes. I met Bruce Fleischer there, who had won the U.S. Amateur as a junior college student. His girlfriend lived in one of my condos.

Mendy and Eleanor, 1970s

Eleanor would have wanted to get married. When I added up all the pluses and the minuses of marriage, I decided I didn't want it. Maybe it was for the best — by the time we broke up, she was on the verge of becoming an alcoholic. We did not part on good terms.

After ten years Frank DePalma moved to the west coast of Florida. My playing partner became Alex Yudow, an avid golfer and resident in one of my condos. I played with him constantly. His brother-in-law was in women's golf apparel, so Alex would get his complimentary tickets for every golf tournament. We went to watch the tournament at Doral every year. Alex also worked as the golf pro on cruise ships whenever he wanted. If I wanted, he could have gotten me that job in his place on cruise ships too when he sat one out, but I knew that I got "mal de mer" when on ships.

I got a letter from Bob Gray with an interesting job offer. One of his clients had plans to open the first Dunkin Donuts, and I could be among the original six people. Bob suggested that I come north to work for the client. But I was too involved with everything in Florida, so I said no thanks. I might have made a lot of money through stock options, but I don't regret it.

The Donners came on vacation a couple of times when Sue and Bill were little. Mike and Dot rented a yacht which they planned to take from Hollywood to the Keys. But a nor'easter storm came up, and they sought shelter in Miami. Then they decided to return and spend their vacation on land. Rose came to visit for a couple of winter months with Aunt Lena. She also came with a girlfriend and rented an apartment in Inverrary in Ft. Lauderdale.

My army buddy Pete had been coming down to Florida from Rockford for a few weeks each winter. Father Forrester, the Catholic chaplain from the 809th, would come to visit also. Pete had been an altar boy for him in upper Manhattan in his youth. Once, early on in the war in North Africa, Father Forrester gathered the troops together for a mass and called out if there was anyone who could assist him. To his surprise, his old altar boy Pete stood up and went forward. When they came to visit each year, we had our routine: we would go to the races in the afternoon, and to the clubs at night. Father Forrester on these visits passed as a civilian. He travelled the world and knew many celebrities. He was a world-class freeloader. Once, while at my apartment, he called Mayor Alioto of San Francisco to wish him a happy new year and didn't offer to pick up the tab. He came to the reunions every year.

In September, 1979, the 809th was having a reunion at the Oak N' Spruce resort in the Berkshires. Pete and I let them know we were coming that year, for the first time since the first reunion in 1947. Later some guys told us that they came just because they heard Pete and I were coming. There was a big lawn in front of the main building. A lot of guys in the lounge were watching out the big windows for us on Friday evening, and when we came walking up the lawn, they shouted, "Here they come!" When we entered the room we were engulfed by everyone. You can imagine these men in their 60's and 70's crying and hugging each other after 33 years. I recognized all the guys but one, who was shrunken and white-haired. There was a lot of reminiscing and toasting.

809th Reunion, Lenox, MA, 1980 (Pete Caputi third from left)

809th Reunion, Lenox, MA, 1980

My greatest achievement at the Hallandale post office was that I brought the union in and improved the welfare of everyone. The postmaster there was a tyrant and did whatever he wanted to anyone. In 1965, with my friend Fred Vanderhoff, who was a rebel like me, we contacted the National Association of Letter Carriers and got them involved and used the Miami contract as a model. Nobody had thought of that before. The postmaster protested in vain. For several nights after work Fred and I negotiated the work contract with the postmaster and assistant postmaster. That completely changed how things were run. Now people from Miami and even Washington, D.C. were involved, and things went smoothly after that. The postmaster now treated people with respect and all grievances were resolved. We would renegotiate a new contract every year. In 1971 we merged with the Miami branch, which now consists of all of southern Florida and is one of the largest in the country.

UNCLE MENDY

6
Retirement Years

I RETIRED IN 1982 at age 62. I wanted to have control of my time and be able to do what I wanted, when I wanted. On the day I retired I went to the Buick dealer and bought a Regal, my first new car since my very first car 36 years before. It was a blue two-tone. Previously I had only bought used cars from friends. I lived across from Gulfstream Park. Pete also retired in the early '80's and got an apartment in Hollywood, Florida. We were friends with Arthur H. Warner, a horse trainer now in the Canadian Horse Racing Hall of Fame. In the winter we would go over to Gulfstream during its four-month meet at 7 a.m., to watch them train the horses and to socialize. We frequently hung out at his 60-foot double-wide mobile home in Hollywood. We talked sports, and tried to stump each other with questions. He would always take us to dinner at a nearby seafood restaurant.

One year Art was very excited about one horse he had that was running in the Queen's Plate, which was like the American Kentucky Derby. He flew us up to Woodbine racetrack in Toronto and put us up at a hotel for a week so we could share his proudest moment with him. He footed all the bills. The horse lost. Our being there helped to console him. Arthur had a reputation for babying the horses and taking great care of them.

I golfed with Alex Yudow five days a week, usually in the afternoon. I entered the Senior Olympics in Broward County. I won trophies in basketball, for foul shooting, and in golf, "closest to the hole," which would be held on a short par 3. Other than golf, I never really exercised until years later, after I broke my hip.

Mendy, Shirley Gray (at center) at Keeneland Racetrack, Lexington, KY, 1982

In 1982 Bob Averill, the office manager from Heller's, came for a vacation to Ft. Lauderdale. We went out to dinner at the Yankee Clipper hotel every night he was there, then we would go into the bar. That's where I met Christy, the barmaid. She was a graduate of Carnegie-Mellon with a degree in creative writing. She supported herself working there while trying to become a writer.

Christy was beautiful, with long brown hair. We hit it off together and started dating. We were very, very compatible. She was 34 years old. I looked way younger than my true age. When I told her my age, she said, "Oh good, I like older men." I had my work cut out handling someone who was my intellectual superior.

One morning I took Christy to Gulfstream to meet Art Warner. I took her around and introduced her to everyone, and I could see her eyes open wide at everything she was seeing. She got out her notebook and began talking to the trainers, the grooms, and the hot walkers, who walk the horses to cool down after they are washed. I brought her out there the next day, and she continued talking to everyone and taking notes. We went into the tack room where the workers lived, and she interviewed them. She put in eight hours doing this on the two visits.

A few weeks later she gave me her story titled "Life on the Backstretch." I proofread it. She went to the Ft. Lauderdale Sun-Sentinel and sold them the story.

Mendy and Christy, 1980's

The first installment ran in the Sunday newspaper, and the second installment on Monday. From then on she was in at the newspaper, and they bought anything she wrote.

In 1988 I moved up to Lake Worth, and I was practically commuting 50 miles down to Ft. Lauderdale. It just became too much, and Christy and I said goodbye to each other.

Rose, Merv, Mendy and Milt, Ft. Kent, ME, 1984

On Friday of Labor Day weekend in 1984, a group from our family made a pilgrimage back to Ft. Kent, Maine. There were ten of us, including Rose, Merv, Milt and Shirley, Hillel, Martha and Rick, Debby Bloom, and a few of their children. We flew from Boston to Presque Isle and rented two station wagons. The town clerk had been notified that we were coming, so she had out the big books with all the birth, death and marriage records from the 1910's and '20's at the town hall. I learned that I had been celebrating my birthday on the wrong day. Merv and Milt found out that their mother had had a daughter who had lived only a few days.

None of our houses was there anymore. We found the spot where the shul had stood. It had been destroyed in 1934. Aunt Fannie's father Hillel Klein had transported a huge rock to the site and put a plaque on the rock to commemorate the shul. We held a little religious service there on Saturday for the first time in 50 years. On Sunday we went into the forest on the Allagash River. Milt and one of the younger boys took a canoe ride on the river and overturned into the water. On the way back Milton had chest pains, and when he got home he needed double bypass heart surgery. I stayed with Milt and Shirley for a month to help him rehab.

In 1986 I saw the film "E.T." in a movie theater. It was filled with seniors talking and noisy kids running around while the film played. I swore I wouldn't go to a movie theater again, and I haven't. I watch no TV show that has a laugh track and have worn out my remote's mute button on commercials.

The Donners had moved to Wellington, and I visited them on weekends. Mike had stopped driving, and I would chauffeur him on his various errands and appointments. Once we stopped at McDonald's for lunch, the only time I have ever been in one. I have eaten in Wendy's and Pizza Hut.

In 1988, my sister Dot was looking for a winter rental for a friend. I went along with her since I had nothing else to do, and we came to look at The Fountains in Lake Worth. We were shown a furnished condo for sale for $37,000, "as is." I told the agent, "I'll take it." I knew I would eventually move up here — for years I had looked at new construction from Boca on north. Once I looked at a townhouse model at Boca West which was selling for $25,000 furnished. Today it goes for $300,000.

I moved up to The Fountains in 1988. I went to The Fountains country club to see about joining. I became a social member, which meant I could play in the afternoon, walking. My apartment backed up against the 1st fairway, and on the other side was the driving range. At the end of the day when the truck would scoop up balls, I'd take a 9-iron and hit balls from the periphery toward the middle of the range. Over the years I hit thousands of balls. I was once scheduled to play with Jack Handelsman, who was a member, but he was told he could not bring a non-equity resident as a guest. There was great animosity between equity and non-equity residents.

The second summer I joined nearby Palm Beach National, a private country club owned by Bob Rich, a Fortune 500 executive. I got in with the men's group who were running club tournaments and other club events. We were a committee of five. When any course in South Florida was renovated or a new course built, it had to be measured and rated again for handicap purposes for USGA approval. Our committee was appointed to do the rating and measurement of courses in south Florida for the Florida State Golf Association, an affiliate of the USGA.

Some of these courses we worked were ultra-private and restricted. The managers kowtowed to us since they needed our services. Among the conditions included in the job were lunch when we finished, and an agreement to play the course at a later date. We would work measuring or rating for three or four hours, have lunch at the club, and then we would come back and play the course another day. One of our most memorable jobs found five Jewish men resplendent in their blue blazers dining with the manager at table #1 at the restricted, exclusive Everglades Club, which once had refused membership to Joseph Kennedy, because he was a Catholic.

There are 125 golf courses in Palm Beach County alone, so we worked almost every week. I also helped run the weekly tournaments at Palm Beach National. I was in the money almost every week at the tournaments, and with the prizes of gift certificates for the pro shop which I won, I acquired an extensive wardrobe of shirts, pants, and golf shoes.

Another highlight of retired life was my work at a professional Mini Golf Tour. In 1990, a New York entrepreneur decided that south Florida needed a Mini Tour for aspiring golf pros. He had heard about our ratings committee, so he hired two of us to work for the Gold Coast Mini Tour. With so many golf clubs around, each with a few pros, there were plenty of players. He arranged the dates for three-day midweek tournaments. They were co-ed the first year. I would arrive each day at 7:00 a.m. and act as the starter, ranger and forecaddy, make rulings and take care of problems. We used walkie-talkies to communicate with each other, and each man had his own golf cart. With business slow in the summer, we had access to many private and exclusive clubs for our tournaments. The tour fed and beveraged us, and we had future playing privileges.

The next year there were 140 men and 50-60 women, so the tour divided into two groups. I went alone with the women. I ran the tour of 18 to 20 weekly tournaments and acted as the starter, ranger, rules official, confidant, and father figure. I announced each player at the first tee in my stentorian voice. I became very friendly with all the young women, we kidded around, and I gave them encouragement. After the tournaments, I would spend a long time talking with some of them. Many of the girls had an interesting history. One was Debbie Denniger, whose grandfather had founded McGregors, my brother-in-law Murray's employer. One girl had been the Canadian amateur champ, and another had gone to Colby College near Claremont.

This went on for several years, until Jack Nicklaus saw how successful we were, and he decided to create some competition. He could offer more in prize money from sponsors. So in 1994, the owner of the tour announced that it would be ending. On my birthday in September that year, the girls brought me a birthday cake out to the first tee. I was moved that these young apparently hard-boiled golf pros would do such a thing. All but one were under age 30, and underneath they were really sentimental.

After the last tournament, everyone got together in the

clubhouse one last time. The girls had pooled their money and bought gifts for each person who worked for the tour. They gave the other guys small gifts like a sleeve of golf balls. They saved me for last. When they called me up to the podium, they gave me a standing ovation. They presented me with a golf cap which they had all autographed. I gave a little speech, and then they gave me another standing ovation. When I returned to my table, the other guys were a little pissed off. "How do you do it?" one of them asked.

I still have my notes from my speech to them. Part of it read: "Always remember this: in the end, the only thing that will really matter is that you will be able to look back and say, I gave it my best shot. Don't ever settle for less."

Then a week later, the thank-you notes started arriving. I still have about 20 of them in an envelope. One of the women wrote, "I hope spending five months with 40 competitive women wasn't too intimidating for you!" The women were so thoughtful. The men wouldn't even have said thank you.

The next year I was treated for prostate cancer. I had to go for radiation treatment five days a week for seven weeks for the prostate cancer. I went in every afternoon with a big smile and kept my cheery outlook. Some of the other patients were feeling sorry for themselves and full of self-pity. I was able to keep playing golf and did not have any side effects. I surprised the office and radiation attendants on my last day by presenting them with a huge floral and goodie basket. No one else had ever given them a thank-you gift.

I took a week off in the middle of the treatment to go to the USGA Rules School. It was from 9:00 to 4:00 for a week, at PGA National in Palm Beach Gardens. We studied the 84-page rulebook sentence by sentence, together with the 1,000 page book of rulings. In addition to classes, we went out on the course and got into the practical situations with the instructor placing balls down from tee to bunker to green and asking us what the ruling would be in various situations. The instructor was the head of the women's USGA section. Once with a ball in the bunker, she spent a very long time going over all the possibilities. She asked me what I would do. I made them all laugh by saying, "I would wave the next group through." On Friday, there was a difficult 100-question test, open book so you were like an official on the course. I scored a very good 87 and have my certificate.

Palm Beach National was losing money, so the board voted to allow the public to play for $25 a round in the summer. When we figured out what we members were paying, it came to $50 a round. I protested, but they just said that's the way it is. So I quit the club. I played my final round at age 80 and scored a 39 for nine holes. After that, I found I really didn't miss it.

Beginning in 1982, I began going to the 809th reunions. Pete and I would go north to the reunions together each year. We would fly to Providence on a Tuesday, rent a car, then drive to New Bedford, Massachusetts to visit Joe Alberski, who owned a filling station and was losing his sight. We would go to Joe's favorite Chinese restaurant and sleep over. On Wednesday we might tour historic Cape Cod and have lunch at the Daniel Webster Inn. Some years we would go to Newport, Rhode Island. Joe was a skilled amateur chef, and we would buy quehogs in the New Bedford harbor. That evening he would cook us an unbelievable seafood dinner. His wife Gert had worked for Titleist for 40 years.

Back (L to R) Rae, Ely, Rose, Shirley, Mendy, Roz, Merv
Front (L to R) Mike, Dorothy, Murray, 1995

On Thursday morning we would drive to Providence to see Georgie Mollo for lunch. His wife would have the table groaning with Italian snacks. Then we would drive on to Hartford to see Jim Halfpenny, a retired bank trust officer. He would serve us the equivalent of a Thanksgiving turkey dinner, which he had spent the entire day preparing. We would stay at his house that night or at a motel. Halfpenny was a real easy-going guy, but his wife was a religious nut. Our annual visit with him was the highlight of his year.

On Friday morning, Pete, Joe and I would drive the three hours to the reunion in the Poconos at Pocmont resort in Bushkill, Pennsylvania. Looking at the reunion photos, I see that the number attending diminished every year due to deaths. Some now came in wheelchairs. Some brought three generations of their families. Pocmont was on the Poconos entertainment circuit, so there was Friday and Saturday night entertainment, usually a singer and a comedian.

Our last reunion for the whole 809th battalion was in 1996. For another five years, B Company alone continued to gather. Our last reunion was on September 8-10, 2001. Only five guys attended with their families in Albany, New York. I flew up and hooked up with Don Knox. Then because of the attack on the World Trade Center on 9/11, I couldn't fly home for a few days because all the planes were grounded. I stayed at my nephew David Feldman's house until I could go home. My great-nephew Matthew was in the fourth grade, and we got to know each other very well that week. I think I've had the knack of talking to kids by putting myself into their age bracket. There's no age limit to humor. I was touched when years later he wrote about me for his college entrance essay, which I'm sure was the deciding factor in his acceptance at the University of Pennsylvania. In it he said I was his idol.

A few years ago I put on my army cap and blouse again and went to a Veterans Day ceremony in Wellington. I didn't stand up when they played "God Bless America," and afterwards people came over and asked me why not. I replied, "It's not the national anthem. It's just a pop song

Irving Berlin wrote to make money." My blouse adorned with all my ribbons and medals is probably what prevented any mayhem.

UNCLE MENDY

7
Encore

SOME YEARS AGO I woke up and my vision out of my right eye was gone. It only saw black. The doctors think I probably had a mini-stroke in it. So since then, I've had sight in only one eye, which means I have no depth perception.

I was watching the Breeders' Cup on television in November, 2006, and between races I was going across the parking lot to see my friend in the next building. As I was going down the three steps out front, with no depth perception, I stepped off the edge of one, fell, and landed on my right hip, breaking it. My friend Joe called 911, and I went to the hospital for a hip replacement.

Then I went to rehab for four weeks at the Hyatt Lakeside in Lantana, located at the complex where Dot lived. I began therapy. Since I could not bend, I had a device to pull up my socks, and a picker-upper to reach things on the floor. I would wheel myself all over in my wheelchair, sometimes breaking the speed restrictions, in my Red Sox cap, which I always wore. Because my breakfast would arrive at my room cold, I got permission to eat breakfast in the dining room. My downstairs friend Joe would bring my mail and other necessities to me from my apartment.

I was the only one eating in the dining room other than those in intensive nursing. My table for lunch and dinner was the first one on the left inside the dining room, with one other person.

On my second evening they wheeled in a pretty little white-haired woman and placed her at my table. She looked like Audrey Hepburn with short white hair. There were menus for each meal, where you checked off what you wanted. I gave her a menu, and she seemed puzzled, so I knew she needed help. I read off the items for her to select, and occasionally she just said, "I'll have what you're having." We talked, we laughed, and she told me some of her history. I gathered that she had early Alzheimer's.

Her name was Muriel. She mentioned that she had performed in Broadway musicals. I asked her which was her favorite. She said, "Boys and Girls," a show I had never heard of. But with my knowledge of Broadway, it suddenly dawned on me: "Guys and Dolls?" She pointed at me with her finger and said, "That's it!" And that is what she continued to do when I would come up with the answer to what she was trying to think of.

The next morning at breakfast I saw her at a distant table with extreme nursing patients. I asked the server if she would wheel her over to my table next to the kitchen entrance. Muriel arrived with the biggest angelic smile.

We started to have all our meals together. I began to know and order what she liked. We would spend an hour or more at meals eating, talking, and laughing. She was in rehab because she had hurt her leg dancing at a musical activity performance in the neighboring memory support wing where she lived. She had gone to Brooklyn College and then had been a performer singing and dancing on Broadway, usually as a stand-in for the lead. She had been in many musicals in the '50's and '60's, including "Guys and Dolls," "Damn Yankees," "West Side Story," "My Fair Lady," and "Fiddler on the Roof." She was ten years younger than I, and looked even much younger than that.

That first night after dinner, as we wheeled ourselves over to the ice cream parlor, she told me, "You're a lovely man." I'll never forget that. After breakfast we would go to therapy, she looking at me for approval as she did her exercises. I needed my male aide Pierre only to wake me and wash my back. Pierre was from the islands, and we spoke French to each other. I enjoyed the fact that I was still able to remember some French 70 years later.

I improved rapidly. After a few days I knew my routine of exercises and was on my own. Soon I was promoted to a walker. I exceeded the expected pace of recovery, and the therapists kidded around with me. "How old did you say you were?" they would ask. Then I was walking around with my walker outside and after four weeks was discharged. For the next ten days, a therapist visited me at home, supervised my exercising, and arranged for me to have a pedicure bi-monthly since I can't bend down that low. I had grab bars installed.

After I went home I called Muriel every night for the next few weeks. We talked from 7:30 to 9:00 p.m. It's amazing how the conversation just flowed. We would sing together our goodnight song, "I'll See You in My Dreams." When I was with her and talking with her, she appeared and sounded normal. One would never have known she had Alzheimer's. During one of our conversations she told me she was leaving soon but didn't know where. I told her, "Wherever you go, I'll find you."

Suddenly after a few weeks, I called one night and was told she was gone. I went over to Lakeside and asked all around, but nobody would or could tell me. There is a Florida law that patient information can only be given to immediate family. Finally one of the nurses I'd been friendly with slipped me a piece of paper with the word, "Encore." I went home and looked in the phone book. I found Encore Senior Living, an Alzheimer's care residence. It was located on Jog Road, right across the street from The Fountains. I went over there, and there was Muriel sitting outside in a chair as if asleep. I went over to her and started singing, "I'll See You in My Dreams." She opened her eyes, and smiled, "You found me!"

I was given the gate code, and from then on I went over there every morning. I would bring her a cookie or a chocolate. We would walk in the garden or sit on the porch and talk and laugh and sing and dance. There were activities there each morning and afternoon: musical performances, monthly birthday celebrations, and a rabbi would come on Friday afternoon to hold a service. I found out that as her visitor, I was entitled to one free meal a day, so our routine included me joining her either for lunch or dinner. I made and took her to beauty parlor appointments. She still remembered all the melodies to songs from her career. We would sing together, and play Name that Tune, where one of us would hum a song for the other to guess the name. She knew 99% of the melodies to the top 20 songs from the '30's, '40's and '50's. She called me, "my man." I called her "sweetie-pie."

Muriel was the happiest Alzheimer's patient alive. At first she did not participate at the daily activities but just sat and listened. Then she started to get into them with me, eventually dominating when the group would sing, imagining she was on stage. She would go up and sing next to the entertainer, and her face was animated. The traveling rabbi organized a seder each year in the main room where the kitchen was. When I told her we were going, she jumped up and went to her wardrobe to try to decide what she would wear. At the seder, she sat next to the rabbi and sang in full voice some of the songs in the Hagadah she still knew by heart. The rabbi, who was on the nursing home circuit, probably never had this happen before.

Muriel's sister came to visit and told me she marveled that Muriel was not deteriorating and seemed so normal. I stimulated her mind by letting her make decisions on everything we did. She greeted her son with a hug on his visits, and she was so happy that he thanked me for spending my time with her. He told me that he had expected a different reception from her. But finally her son moved her north to be close to him in New Jersey, because her deterioration was eventually certain. So we had two years together. She often said they were the happiest years of her life. They were the most gratifying years for me.

8
My Own Ticket

MRS. HUTCHEON, WHO had worked at Heller's, told a Scottish joke about a woman who was walking her three children down the street and met someone who had not seen her in a long time, who said, "Are these your children?" The lady replied, "Yes." "Oh, I didn't know you were married!" "I'm not," said the mother of the children, "but neither have I been neglected!"

I can say that I have not been neglected. I've had quite varied relationships with beautiful women with great personalities. My relation with Muriel was ethereal, while my relations with the others were earthy. They all loved me and liked my humor. I was always a one-woman man, and I was 100% faithful 100% of the time. I feel like I've had five long honeymoons. I regret that some didn't last longer, but maybe then I would not have met the others. That's not bad compared to so many people I've known, who were unhappily married to each other for 40 or 50 years, leading lives of quiet desperation.

When I was young in Claremont, my favorite film actress was Rochelle Hudson. She had a beautiful face, with kind of a square jaw, and appeared mostly in B pictures. I think that the women I've loved have maybe resembled her. Later my favorite became Audrey Hepburn. I've watched "Holiday in Rome", "Breakfast at Tiffany's", and "Love in the Afternoon" each a number of times on TCM.

I really admire the actress Maria Bello. I think she is the best dramatic actress in film today — and I have seen a lot of films. I watched her play a doctor in the fourth season of "E.R." on TV. She starred in "The Cooler" and "A History of Violence."

A few years ago, I bought her a birthday card, signed it "MB", wrote my phone number on it, and sent it to the address on her website. I guess the public relations company that screens the mail passed it on to her, thinking it was from someone she knew. One night I got a phone call from her, curious to know who the card was from. I pointed out to her that we had the same initials. We talked for a while.

Thus began a series of phone conversations which continues to this day. We call each other every month or so. She went to Villanova thinking of becoming a politician. But she took a drama class and found a home. She is very active in liberal political causes. She has been given awards from various activist organizations, like the ACLU. One night she called very upset that a prisoner was being executed in California. We stayed on the line a long time, and I think I helped her. Lately she has been working in a hospital in Haiti helping earthquake victims.

Maria has the highest integrity in her profession. She does not have to be the star of the film, but she wants to play a meaty role. She is not the typical Hollywood type. She writes her own ticket.

If we had met each other when I was younger, we could have had a great relationship.

My favorite artist is Norman Rockwell. Every picture he painted told a story. Accordingly, I hate abstracts. As for sports figures, I admired Ted Williams. I forgave him his transgressions, that he was not a very good husband or father, but he always gave it his best on the field. He was no showboat. When he hit a home run, he didn't stand and admire it, but rather he ran around the bases at top speed. Without publicity, he constantly visited kids in hospitals and orphanages. He did not notify photographers and reporters first like some others did. To me, heroes are those who do great deeds of goodness without seeking or wanting publicity.

Dorothy, Mike, Amy, Mendy and Pam

I've always had good relations with my brothers-in-law and relatives. I was objective and never judgmental. I minded my own business and never interfered with theirs.

Mendy, Adam, Mike, and Matt

One regret might be that I didn't go to Israel with Papa when he went there in the 1950's. It was the realization of his dream as a Zionist to travel there. I helped him buy some lightweight suits for the trip, but I was too busy to go along with him. I could have been there to help him on the trip. I still use Papa's wallet, which has got to be 80 years old. I've patched it innumerable times. And I still use his umbrella. After all these years, the handle of the umbrella is a little broken, but it still works fine.

Dan, Mendy, David, 1999

Looking back on it all now, I feel satisfied with my life. I didn't live worrying or caring about what other people thought about me, or about what I should or should not be doing. You could say I wrote my own ticket.

UNCLE MENDY

Blumberg cousins. Row 1: Pam, Rae, Mendy, Marti   Row 2: Lewis, David F., Dan, David S., Bill, Susan, Skytop, PA, 2009

Blumberg Family Reunion, Skytop, PA, 2009

Dan, Mendy, David, 90th birthday, 2009

Gray cousins. Giela, Hillel, Rena, Debby, Martha, Steve, Shelley, Carol

The Fountains, Trevi Court, Lake Worth, FL

Afterword

APRIL 2010

TO BE CLOSER to the family, Mendy decided he would try out living in independent senior housing in central New Jersey, but just for the summer and fall. He insisted he would be a snowbird and return to Florida for the winter. I flew down to Florida to accompany him on the trip north.

When I arrived at his one-bedroom condo, he wanted to make me dinner, to use up what was left in his refrigerator so nothing would go to waste. He made me a turkey sandwich on the two remaining pieces of bread in the house and heated up his last package of frozen French fries in the toaster oven. The best part of the meal was a can of Boston baked beans. This was his payment of a wager to me on the NHL hockey playoffs, since the Flyers had beaten the Bruins. If it had gone the other way, I would have owed him a Philadelphia cheesesteak. I could not get him to throw out the quarter-full bottles of condiments in his refrigerator, though. That would have been wasteful. But how can you argue with a man who knew the scarcity of food during the Depression and during the freezing winter campaign in Italy in World War II?

The next day we finished taping up his nine large boxes, and the UPS man came for pick-up. Next on his to-do list was disconnecting the battery cable in his car to preserve the battery for 5 months. The cable was stuck on, and after yanking at it with a wrench under the hood in the 98-degree heat, we finally drove to a gas station, where the attendant was able to loosen it. That is, Uncle Mendy drove, this being Florida. He didn't drive badly for a guy with only one working eye and one working ear.

Next it was time to close and secure the hurricane shutters on his windows. They too seemed not to have moved in a great while and were stuck. We finally got them to shut, after knocking off the wasp nest which had been built on the window ledge. Fortunately, it contained only one wasp.

When we went to the UPS store to pay, we were told that a bottle in one of the boxes must have opened or broken, because the box was wet. What is that, I asked Uncle Mendy? He confessed it was a partial bottle of balsamic vinegar he was shipping north to his new kitchen. He hadn't wanted it to go to waste.

The next morning at airport security was a half-hour of misunderstanding as they searched this spry 90-year-old. It began with the metal in his hip replacement, and then his carry-on suitcase also set off an alarm. The guards opened it and found his large metal magnifying glass used for reading, which they suspected was the culprit. But they also discovered a large tube of contraband toothpaste that he failed to keep out and display in a plastic bag. He told me he learned from his flight last year not to take his mouthwash aboard (he had shipped that up in a UPS box), but he hadn't known about the toothpaste. Finally, this World War II vet was found to pose no threat to national security.

A few months later, Mendy reported that he was enjoying his new temporary home. Men were a distinct minority, and he was assigned to a dinner table with seven women. He was charming them each night, and I was sure he would soon have a special lady-friend.

His only complaint was that they were serving him way too much food, more than he could eat. It was wasteful.

APRIL 2011

THE NEXT SPRING, I flew down to West Palm Beach again to bring Uncle Mendy back to New Jersey, this time permanently. He would now reside at that same senior independent living residence, acting as if he were its mayor.

Now, after 64 years in the Sunshine State, he was finally coming north to be closer to family. 64 years of golf and palm trees, the racetrack and the beach. 64 years of the Palm Beach Post. He still took the time to read the entire newspaper each day, which in his view was far superior to the Newark Star Ledger. Each morning he eagerly retrieved the Post from the catwalk balcony that ran the length of the third floor in front of the apartment doors. The delivery man flipped the paper up from ground level, and Mendy recalled once finding the paper "perfectly balanced atop the railing, defying physics."

We taped up his last couple of boxes together. When we took them to the UPS office, he was clearly proud that he did a much better taping job than most other people.

Uncle Mendy made us breakfast. He had geared his consumption to provide that we would have precisely four eggs left on the last day. I sneaked a look at the date on the egg carton to make sure they were okay, as I also did for the can of soup he heated up for our lunch.

The buyers of his car came by with a Department of Motor Vehicles form for him to sign. They were thrilled with their purchase for $1,000 of his 1996 Chrysler with only 27,000 miles on it. Part of the reason for its pristine condition was that nobody had ever sat in the back seat. He was a little sad that he would never drive again, but "I never had an accident."

He had a list of errands to run, and we took care of them one by one. After UPS we went to the AT&T store to shut off his service. But it turned out they only deal in cell phones; he had to call an 800 number after all. Next, we went to the bank to deposit the cash from the sale of the car. Then to Comcast to turn in his cable box. Then back to the bank a second time, because he found a few dollars in quarters, and he wanted to exchange them for bills. Florida has the most patient of bank tellers.

We left his one-bedroom condo at The Fountains for sale at Florida's rock-bottom real estate price of $25,000. While I was there helping him pack, a house-hunter visited and tried to bargain him down a little. Uncle Mendy stood firm: "This isn't Christmas," he reminded the potential buyer, "and I'm giving it to you furnished," as if that were some kind of plus. The woman looked around at the same furniture and the same pictures on the wall which he inherited when he moved in 28 years ago. I read her thoughts as she calculated how much she would have to pay someone to clear out the place.

"Au revoir" to Florida, 2011

On his last morning in Florida, as he returned from the garbage chute and opened his front door for the last time, the Palm Beach Post hit him squarely in the back. He laughed and leaned over the railing to look down for the delivery man, but he was already gone.

Mendy moved north in April, 2011, and spent a happy year and a half at Lester Senior Living in Whippany, NJ. But in late 2012, he suffered a stroke and was confined to his bed and a wheelchair for the last two years of his life. His nephews David Feldman and Dan Schwartz, and even more so their wives, Amy and Judy, devoted huge amounts of time to caring for him, shopping for him, and managing his professional care.

For his 95th birthday, some of his nephews, nieces, and their families, and his sister Rae gathered around his bedside. Although he had lost his ability to speak, his face conveyed his joy for the love of those who surrounded him.

Uncle Mendy passed away in February of 2015. He was buried at Cedar Park and Beth-El Cemetery in Paramus, NJ. His gravestone reads:

Beloved Brother and Uncle
Mendel "Mendy" Blumberg
Sept. 26, 1919 – Feb. 11, 2015
Indomitable   Authentic   Admired

About The Author

DAVID SCHWARTZ spent his career as a Philadelphia lawyer. In retirement he pursues his life-long interest in history as a volunteer park ranger and walking tour guide at Independence National Historical Park. He lives with his wife Maryellen in the historic Naval Square neighborhood.

He is the author of a novel, *Elsewhere Than Vietnam: A Story of the Sixties*, based on his experiences in the U.S. Army. He is also the author of *A VIP Day at Independence Park*, a behind-the-scenes tour of Independence National Historical Park.

www.ingramcontent.com/pod-product-compliance
Lightning Source LLC
Chambersburg PA
CBHW071517040426
42444CB00008B/1680